Our American Holidays

INDEPENDENCE DAY

INDEPENDENCE DAY

ITS CELEBRATION, SPIRIT, AND SIGNIFICANCE
AS RELATED IN PROSE AND VERSE

EDITED BY

ROBERT HAVEN SCHAUFFLER

NON-IN
FERIOR
A SEQV
ENTES

NEW YORK
MOFFAT, YARD AND COMPANY
1915

Republished by Omnigraphics • 615 Griswold Street • Detroit • 2000

Library of Congress Cataloging-in-Publication Data

Independence Day : its celebration, spirit, and significance as
related in prose and verse / edited by Robert Haven
Schauffler.
    p.   cm. — (Our American holidays)
    Reprint : New York : Dodd, Mead, and Co., 1926.
    ISBN 0-7808-0394-9
    1. Fourth of July Literary collections. 2. United States—
History—Revolution, 1775–1783 Literary collections.
3. United States. Declaration of Independence Literary
collections. 4. American Literature. I. Schauffler, Robert
Haven, 1879–1964. II. Series.
PS509.F63I54   1999
810.8′0334—dc21   99-28344
                                                               CIP

Printed in the United States of America

CONTENTS

CONTENTS

III

BEFORE THE DAWN OF INDEPENDENCE

IV

THE DECLARATION

CONTENTS

V

THE STRUGGLE FOR INDEPENDENCE

VI

SWEET LAND OF LIBERTY

CONTENTS

VII

FICTION

VIII

THE NEW FOURTH

PREFACE

THIS book is an anthology of American Independence: of the document that announced its birth; of the struggle that established it in life; and of the patriotism that was to it both sire and son. It aims to present a clear review of the origin, spirit and significance of Independence Day and of its celebration both by the now discredited methods of brutal, meaningless noise and indiscriminate carnage, which disgraced the larger part of the previous century, and by the recent methods of sane and safe, reverent and meaningful celebration.

The volume contains a selection of the best prose and verse that bears in any way on our nation's birthday; and closes with many constructive suggestions for the celebration of our new, more beautiful and more patriotic Fourth.

NOTE

THANKS are due to Miss Jessie Welles, superintendent of circulation in the Carnegie Library, Pittsburgh, for the suggestion which originated " Our American Holidays." And gratitude is also expressed to the Misses Tobey, to Miss Helen Miles and all the other librarians of the Bloomingdale Branch Library in New York who have generously given the editor such invaluable aid in the preparation of these volumes.

The Editor also wishes to acknowledge his indebtedness to Houghton, Mifflin & Company; The Century Co.; J. B. Lippincott & Co.; Bobbs-Merrill Co., and others who have very kindly granted permission to reprint selections from works bearing their copyright.

ROBERT HAVEN SCHAUFFLER.

INTRODUCTION

WHEN, on the fourth day of each July, Americans keep the birthday of the nation we celebrate as our greatest secular holiday, the one which has the honor of being sanctioned by statute in every state of the Union.

From times as early as any living memory can reach, this anniversary has been observed in much the same fashion: by spread-eagle oratory, by unlimited and quite meaningless noise, and hospitals filled with the wounded and dying. It is curious that the festival should have gone on in this monotonous manner decade after decade until nearly the middle of its second century of life, and then suddenly should have encountered a revolution far more abrupt than the early, heroic one which it commemorates.

For our attitude toward the Fourth is undergoing swift revolution as regards our understanding both of the causes that underlay American independence, of the real spirit in which the Declaration was penned, and of the reasons why July fourth rather than some other day was fixed upon. Finally, the swiftest Fourth of July revolution of all is taking place in the way we celebrate it.

Until quite recently all historians have, consciously or unconsciously, been consistent in misrepresenting the War of Seventy-Six and the events leading thereto. And we owe no small debt of gratitude to writers like Mr. Owen Wister and Mr. Sydney

George Fisher for telling us the truth. Mr. Wister writes [1] of the Revolution that while " As a war, its real military aspect is slowly emerging from the myth of uninterrupted patriotism and glory, universally taught to school children, its political hue is still thickly painted and varnished over by our writers.

" How many Americans know, for instance, that England was at first extremely lenient to us? fought us (until 1778) with one hand in a glove, and an olive branch in the other? had any wish rather than to crush us; had no wish save to argue us back into the fold, and enforce argument with an occasional victory not followed up? . . . For any American historian to speak the truth on these matters is a very recent phenomenon, their common design having been to leave out any facts which spoil the political picture of the Revolution they chose to paint for our edification: a ferocious, blood-shot tyrant on the one side, and on the other a compact band of ' Fathers,' downtrodden and martyred, yet with impeccable linen and bland legs. A wrong conception even of the Declaration of Independence as Jefferson's original invention still prevails; Jefferson merely drafted the document, expressing ideas well established in the contemporary air. Let us suppose that some leader of our own time were to write: ' Three dangers to-day threaten the United States, any one of which could be fatal: unscrupulous capital, destroying man's liberty to compete; unscrupulous Labor, destroying man's liberty to work; and undesirable Immigration, in which four years of naturalization are not going to counteract four hundred years of heredity. Unless the people check all of these, American liberty will become ex-

[1] *In " The Seven Ages of Washington."*

tinct.' If some one were to write a new Declaration of Independence, containing such sentences, he could not claim originality for them; he would be merely stating ideas that are among us everywhere. This is what Jefferson did, writing his sentences loosely, because the ideas they expressed were so familiar as to render exact definitions needless."

Mr. Wister deserves gratitude for giving us these unpalatable truths in such palatable form; but he should have far more gratitude for introducing to a wide body of readers his chief source of information, the historian Mr. Sydney George Fisher, one of whose most valuable chapters has fortunately been secured for reproduction in the body of this book. Mr. Fisher writes:[1]

"I cannot feel satisfied with any description of the Revolution which treats the desire for independence as a sudden thought, and not a long growth and development, or which assumes that every detail of the conduct of the British government was absurdly stupid, even from its own point of view, and that the loyalists were few in numbers and their arguments not worth considering. . . .

"The historians seem to have assumed that we do not want to know about that controversy" (over Gen. Howe's lenient methods), "or that it will be better for us not to know about it. They have assumed that it will be better for Americans to think that independence was a sudden and deplorable necessity and

---

[1] *In the Introduction to " The True History of the American Revolution." For the most modern and unvarnished presentation of the inner history of the period see also his larger work, " The Struggle for American Independence." (Lippincott.)*

not a desire of long and ardent growth and cautiously planned intention. They have assumed that we want to think of England as having lost the colonies by failure to be conciliatory, and that the Revolution was a one-sided, smooth affair, without any of the difficulties or terrors of a rebellion or a great upheaval of settled opinion."

There can be small doubt that when this true inner history of our independence becomes generally known it will do much to mitigate the blind, provincial spread-eagleism that still clings to even our safest and sanest celebrations of the Fourth and that has so ably thwarted every motion toward fraternal intimacy between the two great branches of the Anglo-Saxon race. The following [1] paragraph is fairly typical of the British attitude toward the celebration of our national birthday.

" Where a country or a government has been baffled in its efforts to attain or preserve a hated rule over another people, it must be content to see its failure made the subject of never-ending triumph and exultation. The joy attached to the sense of escape or emancipation tends to perpetuate itself by periodical celebrations, in which it is not likely that the motives of the other party, or the general justice of the case, will be very carefully considered or allowed for. We may doubt if it be morally expedient thus to keep alive the memory of facts which as certainly infer mortification to one party as they do glorification to another: but we must all admit that it is only natural, and in a measure to be expected."

When we come to view the facts as they are, to realize of what shocking sportsmanship our own one-

[1] *From Chambers' " Book of Days."*

sided view of independence convicts us, we shall have removed one of the chief obstacles to Anglo-Saxon solidarity. But it will be necessary first to learn something about the day we celebrate. How many, for instance, even know that July fourth was fixed upon as a compromise date between two other rival claimants?

Walsh writes:[1]

"It may not be generally known that no less than three dates might reasonably compete for designation as the natal day of American Independence and for the honors of the anniversary of that event.

"On the second of July, 1776, was adopted the resolution of independence, the sufficient legislative act; and it was this day that Mr. Adams designated as the anniversary in the oft-quoted letter written on his desk at the time, prophesying its future celebration, by bells, bonfires, cannonades, etc. On the fourth of July occurred the Declaration of Independence. On the second of August following took place the ceremony of signature, which has furnished to the popular imagination the common pictorial and dramatic conceptions of the event.

"The history connecting these three dates may be intelligently told in a brief space. On the fifteenth of May, 1776, a convention in Virginia had instructed its delegates in the General Congress 'to propose to that body to declare the United Colonies free and independent States, absolved from all allegiance to or dependence on the Crown or Parliament of Great Britain, and that they give the assent of this Colony to such declaration, and to whatever measures may be thought proper and necessary by the Congress for

[1] *In " Curiosities of Popular Customs."*

forming foreign alliances and a confederation of the Colonies.' The motion thus ordered was on the seventh of June made in Congress by Richard Henry Lee, as the oldest member of the Virginia delegation. It was to the effect that 'these United Colonies are, and of right ought to be, free and independent States; that they are absolved from all allegiance to the British crown; and that all political connection between them and the state of Great Britain is, and ought to be, totally dissolved.' The resolution was slightly debated for two or three days, but from considerations of prudence or expediency the discussion was intermitted. As texts for the action of Congress there were the resolution referred to, and the more formal, or at least more lengthy, document which the committee of five — Jefferson, Adams, Franklin, Sherman, and Livingston — had been instructed on the eleventh of June to prepare. This document was draughted by Jefferson and presented under the title of 'A Declaration by the Representatives of the United States of America in General Congress assembled.'

"On the first of July there was again called up in Congress the resolution proposed by Mr. Lee. On the second of July it passed. Two days later (the fourth of July) was adopted, after various amendments, the 'Declaration' from Mr. Jefferson's pen. The document was authenticated, like the other papers of the Congress, by the signature of the president and the secretary, and, in addition, was signed by the members *present,* with the exception of Mr. Dickinson of Pennsylvania, who, as Mr. Jefferson has testified, 're-fused to sign it.'

"But it did not then bear the names of the members

of Congress as they finally appeared on it. A number of these still opposed it, and had voted against it; it was passed unanimously only as regarded states. Thus, a majority of the Pennsylvania delegation had persistently opposed it, and it was only the absence of two of their delegates on the final vote that left a majority for this state in its favor. Some days after the Declaration had thus passed, and had been proclaimed at the head of the army, it was ordered by Congress that it be engrossed on parchment and signed by every member; and it was not until the second of August that these signatures were made, and the matter concluded by this peculiar and august ceremony of personal pledges in the autographs of the members. It is this copy or form of the Declaration which has, in fact, been preserved as the original: the first signed paper does not exist, and was probably destroyed as incomplete.

" If the natal day of American Independence is to be derived from the ceremony of these later signatures, and the real date of what has been preserved as the legal original of the Declaration, then it would be the second of August. If derived from the substantial, legal *act* of separation from the British Crown, which was contained rather in the resolution of Congress than in its Declaration of Independence, it would be the second of July. But common consent has determined to date the great anniversary from the apparently subordinate event of the passage of the Declaration, and thus celebrates the Fourth of July as the birthday of the nation."

Finally, after making ourselves reasonably intelligent as to the origin, spirit and true significance of Independence Day it behooves us as true Americans to enter the splendid new movement which is endeavoring to make the Fourth over from a day of shallow jingoism and unmeaning brutality and carnage into a day of initiation into the meaning of true citizenship and a festival of deep and genuine and beautiful patriotism.

R. H. S.

I
CELEBRATION

INDEPENDENCE DAY

THE GREAT AMERICAN HOLIDAY

ANONYMOUS

AMONG all the holidays of the year, one stands out as preëminently American; one appeals especially to that sentiment of patriotism and national pride which glows in every loyal American heart. Independence Day — the Fourth of July — is observed in every State in the Union as our distinctive national holiday; and rightly so, for the event which it celebrates is by far the most important in American history — an event no less, indeed, than the birth of the nation.

Independence Day celebrates the signing, on the Fourth of July, 1776, of the paper which declared this country forever free from British rule. It had been under consideration for some time by the Continental Congress, assembled at Philadelphia, and final action was finally taken on July 4. From that time forward, the American colonists were no longer rebels in arms against their country, but a free people fighting for their independence.

That the Declaration of Independence was mainly the work of Thomas Jefferson has been established beyond reasonable doubt; and it stands to-day one of the most remarkable state papers in the history of the world.

At the time of the passage of the act, John Adams wrote to his wife a letter which has become historic. " I am apt to believe," he wrote, " that this day will be celebrated by succeeding generations as the great anniversary festival. It ought to be commemorated as the day of deliverance, by solemn acts of devotion to God Almighty. It ought to be solemnized with pomp and parade, with shows, games, sports, guns, bells, bonfires, and illuminations, from one end of this continent to the other, from this time forward forevermore."

Bonfires and guns there have been without limit; and the deaths that have resulted from these celebrations would form no inconsiderable fraction of those lost during the Revolution. For years, the celebration of this great holiday has consisted mainly of meaningless noise; but there is a steadily growing sentiment in favor of a more worthy observance of the day, as a time when every loyal American should rejoice in the welfare of his country, and recall with pride the manner in which the Nation was established.

THE NATION'S BIRTHDAY

BY MARY E. VANDYNE

Ring out the joy bells! Once again,
  With waving flags and rolling drums,
We greet the Nation's Birthday, when,
  In glorious majesty, it comes.

Ah, day of days! Alone it stands,
   While, like a halo round it cast,
The radiant work of patriot hands,
   Shines the bright record of the past.

Among the nations of the earth,
   What land hath story like our own?
No thought of conquest marked her birth;
   No greed of power was ever shown
By those who crossed the ocean wild,
   That they might plant upon her sod
A home for Peace and Virtue mild,
   And altars rear to Freedom's God.

How grand the thought that bade them roam!
   Those pilgrim bands, by Faith inspired —
That bade them leave their cherished home,
   And, with the martyr's spirit fired,
Guide their frail vessels o'er the main
   Upon the glorious mission bound
On alien soil a grave to gain,
   Or else a free born nation found.

What land has heroes like to ours?
   Their names are as the lightning's gleams,
When, on the darkling cloud that lowers,
   In blinding majesty it streams.
Great Washington, the man of faith,
   Who conquered doubt with patient might;
Warren and Putnam, true till death,
   The " Swamp Fox," eager for the fight.

See Major Molly's woman hand
  Drive home the murderous cannon ball;
How bravely Lydia Darrach planned,
  For home and country risking all.
A glorious list, and without end;
  Forgotten were both sex and age;
Their names in radiant luster blend,
  And shine like stars on history's page.

Like stars to light the firmament,
  And show the world what men may do
Who, as God's messengers, are sent
  And to their mission still are true.
No end had they to seek or gain;
  Their work was there before their sight;
There lay their duty, stern and plain,
  To dare and suffer for the right.

The right that conquered, and whose power
  Is shown in our broad land to-day;
Shown in this bright and prosperous hour,
  When peace and plenty gild our way;
Shown in the glorious song that swells
  The hearts of men from South to North,
And in its rapturous accents tell
  The story of our glorious Fourth.

HOW THE FOURTH OF JULY SHOULD BE CELEBRATED

BY JULIA WARD HOWE

I HAVE been invited to present some hints as to the proper observance of our great national holiday, the Fourth of July, and the false education implied by warlike celebrations in a nation whose corner stone is peace and whose freedom is a standing protest against old-world militarism.

The topic carries me back in thought to days of childhood, when, in my native city of New York, the endless crackling of torpedoes, the explosion of fire-crackers and the booming of cannon, made the day one of joyous confusion and fatigue, culminating in a distant view of the city fireworks sent up from Castle Garden. It then seemed to be a day wholly devoted to boyish pleasure and mischief, sure to be followed by reports of hairbreadth escapes and injuries more or less serious, sometimes even fatal. The day was one of terror to parents, who, while deeming it un-wise to interdict to their sons the enjoyment of gun-powder, dreaded to see them maimed or disfigured for life by some unlooked-for accident. It was not un-common then, nor is it now, to read of some sudden death, some irretrievable blindness or other injury caused by the explosion of a toy cannon or the mis-adventure of some fireworks on " the Fourth," as the day has come to be called.

These were tragical events truly, but they appear less real to me in remembrance than do the laugh-ing faces of my young brothers who were allowed to arrange a small table for their greater convenience on the pavement of ancient Bond Street, a very quiet byway in those days. From this spot went forth a perpetual popping and fizzing, varied by the occasional thud of a double-headed firecracker. Shouts of merriment followed these explosions. The girls within doors enjoyed the fracas from the open win-dows, and in the evening our good elders brought forth a store of Roman candles, blue lights, and rockets. I remember a year, early in the thirties, in which good Gideon Lee, a democratic Mayor of New York, issued an edict prohibitive of all home fireworks. Just as we had settled ourselves in the determination to regard him thenceforth as our natural enemy, the old gentleman's heart failed him, and, living next door to us, he called to say that he would make a few exceptions to the rule for the day, and that we should count among these.

Removing to Boston some ten years later, I found the night of the third of July rendered almost sleepless by the shrill gamut of gunpowder discharges. The ringing of bells and the booming of cannon destroyed the last chance of an early morning nap, and in self-defense most people left their beds and went forth to see what could be seen. This was sometimes a mock procession of the Antiques and Horribles, so called in parody of the Ancient and Honorable Artillery, so well known in and about Boston. Or, one might join the throng on the Common, where a brass band performed popular airs, American and Irish-American. I do indeed recall certain notable performances connected with the usual observance of the National Festival. I was a dweller in Boston when Charles Sumner, then chiefly known as a rising lawyer and incipient philanthropist, was appointed to deliver the Fourth of July oration, and chose for his theme the true grandeur of nations. This grandeur he found entirely in the conquests of peace as opposed to the popular worship of military renown. His audience, composed in part of men in soldier's garb, were but little in sympathy with his views, and I remember the performance as having called forth more irritation than approbation.

These prophetic glimpses of good which seem far from the practical questions of the time do visit earnest souls in this way, like some ray of light from an undiscovered star. The same train of thought, at about the same time, took shape in Mr. Longfellow's fine poem on the Arsenal in Springfield. It may be remembered that the poet was Mr. Sumner's most intimate friend. While the two men held the same views regarding the great questions of the time, Mr. Longfellow's *bonhomie* rendered him very inapt to give offense, while Sumner seemed destined to arouse violent opposition in those from whom he differed.

I remember another Fourth of July at which Edward Everett's measured rhetoric and silver voice held the attention of a numerous assemblage. Mr. Everett was certainly master of the art of graceful oratory, and was always heard with appreciation, even by those who felt little satisfaction in his public career.

One of Ralph Waldo Emerson's finest poems was written for the celebration of the Fourth in his own town of Concord. The two opening lines of this dwell always in my memory:

> " Oh! tenderly the haughty Day
> Fills his blue urn with fire."

But, beautiful as they are, the solemn lesson of the poet exceeds them in interest.

> " United States! the Ages plead,
>   Present and Past in under-song;
> Go, put your creed into your deed,
>   Nor speak with double tongue.

" Be just at home, then write your scroll
Of honor o'er the sea,
And bid the broad Atlantic roll
A ferry of the Free."

Here is a thought picture which we may love to
dwell upon. Emerson, the descendant of the Puri-
tans, himself a transfigured Puritan, reading these
stanzas of his, whose fire is tempered by the weight
of thought, in that old town of Concord, where, in
his own phrase:

"— the embattled farmers stood,
And fired the shot heard round the world."

A fiercer fight was then before us, whose issue is
simply prefigured in the words: " Be just at home."
Surely, we might take this saying for a national
motto, its reminder still needed, though the slave is
freed from the whip and fetter. Of the day on which
our Independence was declared John Adams said:
" It ought to be commemorated as the day of deliverance by solemn acts of devotion to God Almighty.
It ought to be celebrated with pomp and parade, with
shows, games, sports, guns, bells, bonfires, and illuminations, from one end of this continent to the other,
from this time forward forevermore."
These words show how comprehensive was the view
which the old statesman took of a Nation's holiday.
He desired that all classes and all ages should participate in the joy expressed. The time which has
elapsed since his memorable utterance has brought
nothing to diminish this joy. It has however brought
into being a new society for which " pomp and parade,

bells, guns and bonfires " are less available for good than pleasures of a more elevated character. We now desire a celebration which shall speak less to the bodily sense and more to the inner sense. This is because the historic development of the race goes ever forward. John Adams would have had both sober and wild rejoicing over the birth of a new state, representing a new order of things. We stand face to face with the question: How shall we maintain our deliverance from old-world trammels? This freedom which was declared in 1776, what are its conditions, what its true uses?

History is full of paradoxes whose meaning does not lie upon the surface of what we see. Many of these recall the riddle of Samson: "Out of the eater came forth meat, and out of the strong came forth sweetness." Even so, the things that make for peace often come out of contests full of violence and bloodshed, while the elements of anarchy ripen best in the submission enforced by autocratic despotism, the ominous quiet which is sure to be broken by some terrific social cataclysm. In the first instance, which alone concerns our theme, we must remember that the bloodshed came, not of the peaceable principles of eternal justice, but of the effort on the part of tyrants to gainsay and oppose these. It follows from this that in commemorating the events which have had most to do with the liberation of mankind from the yoke of despotism and superstition, we must keep in view these underlying truths which in themselves involve no violence, but the vindication of which may involve great sacrifices of devoted lives.

The fact that our heroes fought for freedom against almost hopeless odds should be brought to mind, and their names should be hallowed in perpetual remembrance. But, if we would crown their conquest, we must give more attention to the good for which they died than to the mere circumstance of their death. The ordinary procedure of mankind is quite the opposite of this. They are proud of the military success, careless of the civic and ethical gain. Even the Christian church accentuates too much the death of its Founder, is too little concerned with the truth for which he really gave his life. A Lent of prayer and fasting, with dramatic repetition of the betrayal and crucifixion of the Blessed One, may merely bring with it suggestions of devotion and gratitude. But far more important would be a Lent of study of the deep meaning of his words and works. It makes one sick at heart to think of the formal rehearsal of great events by those who have no understanding of their true significance, and can therefore claim but a small part in their real benefit.

The parallelisms too of history are very instructive. In the confusions and difficulties of our own time it is useful for us to learn that men in other times have had similar problems to solve, and have found their solutions. It is helpful for us to know that our pure and blameless Washington was, in his day, the subject of malignant slander and mischievous cabal. Our own best public men are liable to the grossest misinterpretations of their utterances and of their measures. Unworthy demagogues to-day will present very dangerous evils in a light attractive to the multitude. This has always been so. No man marches to victory over a bed of roses. The roses crown his perseverances, but the thorns lacerate his bleeding feet. But, with these sad recollections, we must keep in sight the immortal hope sung by the poets, reasoned out by the philosophers, and acted out by earth's saints and heroes, the hope which is justified by the great progress of the ages, the elevation of the natural man into the dignity of the spiritual man.

Elizabeth Barrett Browning, who saw one of the great Italian festivals in which the poet Dante was especially commemorated, saw also the pressing need of wise counsel and brave action throughout the struggling country, and asks what will become of the new Italy if her young men shall " stand still strewing violets all the time? " We may ask too what will become of our new Republic if the hours of its highest festival continue to be occupied with fustian oratory, gunpowder enthusiasm, and the exercise of every poor and mean trade, the sale of toys, bad food, and worse liquor?

Now, I would by no means abridge the childish pleasure of the day, if I could do so. We must allow children the explosion of animal spirits, and they will delight, as some grown-up people will, in much that is irrational. But the day itself is too important to be made one of mere noise and parade. It should be made highly valuable for impressing upon the minds of the young the history of their national liberty, and its cause. Besides our own young people, we have with us the youth of many nations, whose parents have come to our shores, drawn by various hopes of gain and benefit. These children will form an important part of our future body politic, in whose government to-day, their parents are, too, easily able to participate.

The question will be, how to make the Fourth of July a true festival, a national solemnity, without forgetting the claims of the young to be amused, as well as to be instructed. In the first place, I should think that the day might fitly be made one of reunion, by different clubs and associations of culture and philanthropy. Those whose thoughts go deep enough to understand the true conditions of human freedom, might meet and compare their studies and experiences. Very fitly, after such a meeting, each individual of them might seek a group, to whose members he might present a popular statement of the philosophy of freedom. Mothers, who should be the true guardians of peace, might well come together to study all that promotes its maintenance. In gatherings of older children, prize essays might be presented and discussed. I can imagine civic banquets, of a serious and stately character, in which men and women might sit together and pledge each other, in the exhilaration of friendship and good feeling.

I would have processions, but I would have them less military in character, and more pacific in suggestion. Congregations of the various religious confessions might walk in order, headed by their ministers, who should all exchange the right hand of fellowship with each other. I would have no monster concerts, which cannot be fully enjoyed, but divers assemblages, at which music of the highest order should be presented. Letters of greeting should be exchanged between cities and states, and the device of the day should be, " In the Name of the Republic." The history of the war which culminated in our national independence should be amply illustrated by graphic lectures, and possibly by living pictures. Mr. John Fiske has an admirable talent for bringing the past and its heroes as vividly before us as if he himself had seen them but the day before. If it were possible to multiply his valued personality, I would have many sketches given in various places, of the brave struggle of our forefathers and of those who were foremost in it.

"Going out of town to avoid the Fourth," has been a phrase so common in my time that it ceases to awaken attention, and is taken as a matter of course. I cannot indeed wonder that people of refined tastes and sensitive nerves should seek to free themselves from the noise and crowd of the usual observance. The question is whether, with a wiser administration, the same people might not be led to gather, rather than to disperse for the celebration.

How would the following programme answer?

On the evening of the third of July, quiet gatherings in halls or churches, in which the true love of country should be explained and illustrated. How many a name, half or wholly forgotten, would then be recalled from oblivion, and with it the labor and sacrifice of some noble life, some example precious for the community!

The morning of the Fourth to be ushered in by martial music, and a military display sufficient to recall the services of the brave men who gave our fathers liberty. At ten o'clock orations in various public buildings, the ablest speakers of the commonwealth doing their best to impart the lesson of the day. At one a Spartan feast, wholesome and simple. No liquor to be served thereat, and none to be sold during the day. From twelve to half past four in the afternoon, I would have exercises for the children of the public schools, examination of classes in American history, prizes given for essays on historical and patriotic subjects. Later, a gathering in public gardens, and a tea, with fruit and flowers, served for the children of the city. In the evening, the singing of national anthems, *tableaux vivants* and fireworks, and in some form, a pastoral benediction.

To these exercises I would add the signing of a pledge of good citizenship. We take much pains, and not unwisely, to persuade men and women to sign a pledge of total abstinence from alcoholic liquors. But why should we not go further than this, and lead them to pledge themselves to some useful service in the community? This pledge might be either general or particular in its terms, but the act of signing it should imply a disinterested public service of some sort, a participation in some work useful for the health, beauty, or order of the city, without other reward than the badge or button which would represent the agreement entered into. I would have the history of other Republics brought forward on this day, and especially, the heroic struggles of our own time. Among these, I would certainly accord a place to the story of the great-hearted men to whom Italy owes her freedom. And I would if I could compel the attendance of our men and women of fashion upon lectures in which the true inwardness of European society should be exposed, and the danger shown of the follies and luxurious pomp which they delight in imitating, and which, however æsthetically adorned and disguised, are for us to lead in the pathway of moral and intellectual deterioration.

I would have the great political offenses of the century fitly shown, the crimes of Louis Napoleon, the rapacious wars of Germany, France and England, the wicked persecution of the Jews. Now that we are nearing the close of our nineteenth century, it becomes most important for us that its historic record should be truly rehearsed, its great saints and sinners characterized, its wonderful discoveries and inventions explained.

The very meager programme suggested here for our great day may appear to many Utopian and impossible. I shall be glad if it can serve to pave the way for kindred suggestions, to which individual minds may give a broader and more varied scope. Let us unite our efforts in behalf of a suitable and serious honoring of the day in such wise that every heart, old and young, shall have therein its especial joy, and every mind its especial lesson.

I had at one time a plan of my own, of setting apart one day in the year as a Mother's Day. This festival was to be held in the interest of a world's peace, and for quite a number of years it was so observed by groups of women in various parts of the country, while in England and even in far-off Smyrna friends met together, with song, prayer, and earnest discourse to emphasize the leading thought, which was that women, as the mothers of the race, knowing fully the cost of human life, should unite their efforts throughout the world to restrain the horrors of war, and to persuade men to keep the sacred bond of peace. It now occurs to me that we should make our Fourth of July a Mother's, as well as a Father's day. In the public programme of every town throughout our vast Commonwealth, women should have some word to say and some part to play. What we have already seen of their culture and ability is enough to assure us that their participation in such proceedings would intensify their good features and discourage their objectionable ones. And as in the forms of oratory with which we are familiar, much is made of what the world owes to America, we might suggest that our women speakers might especially bring forward the antithesis of this question, in another, viz., What America owes to the world.

II

SPIRIT AND SIGNIFICANCE

ENGLAND AND AMERICA

BY JAMES BRYCE

THIS is a memorable day to Englishmen as well as to Americans. It is to us a day both of regret and of rejoicing: of regret at the severance of the political connection which bound the two branches of our race together, and of regret even more for the unhappy errors which brought that severance about, and the unhappy strife by which the memory of it was embittered. But it is also a day of rejoicing, for it is the birthday of the eldest daughter of England — the day when a new nation, sprung from our own, first took its independent place in the world. And now with the progress of time, rejoicing has prevailed over regret, and we in England can at length join heartily with you in celebrating the beginning of your national life. All sense of bitterness has passed away, and been replaced by sympathy with all which this anniversary means to an American heart.

England and America now understand one another far better than they ever did before. In 1776 there was on one side a monarch and a small ruling caste, on the other side a people. Now our government can no longer misrepresent the nation, and across the ocean a people speaks to a people. We have both come, and that most notably within recent months, to perceive that all over the world the interests of America and of England are substantially the same.

The sense of our underlying unity over against the other races and forms of civilization has been a potent force in drawing us together. It is said that the Fourth of July is a day of happy augury for mankind. This is true because on that day America entered on a course and proclaimed principles of government which have been of profound significance for mankind. Many nations have had a career of conquest and of civilizing dominion: but to make an immense people prosperous, happy, and free is a nobler and grander achievement than the most brilliant conquests and the widest dominion.

THE BIRTHDAY OF THE NATION

(From address delivered July 4, 1851, at laying the cornerstone of the new wing of the Capitol.)

BY DANIEL WEBSTER

THIS is that day of the year which announced to mankind the great fact of American Independence! This fresh and brilliant morning blesses our vision with another beholding of the birthday of our Nation; and we see that Nation, of recent origin, now among the most considerable and powerful, and spreading from sea to sea over the continent.

On the fourth day of July, 1776, the representatives of the United States of America, in Congress assembled, declared that these Colonies are, and ought to be, free and independent States. This declaration, made by most patriotic and resolute men, trusting in the justice of their cause and the protection of Heaven,— and yet not without deep solicitude and anxiety — has now stood for seventy-five years. It was sealed in blood. It has met dangers and overcome them. It has had detractors, and abashed them all. It has had enemies, and conquered them. It has had doubting friends, but it has cleared all doubts away; and now, to-day, raising its august form higher than the clouds, twenty millions of people contemplate it with hallowed love, and the world beholds it, and the consequences that have followed from it, with profound admiration.

This anniversary animates and gladdens all American hearts. On other days of the year we may be party men, indulging in controversies more or less important to the public good. We may have likes and dislikes, and we may maintain our political differences, often with warm, and sometimes with angry feelings. But to-day we are Americans all; nothing but Americans.

As the great luminary over our heads, dissipating fogs and mist, now cheers the whole atmosphere, so do the associations connected with this day disperse all sullen and cloudy weather in the minds and feelings of true Americans. Every man's heart swells within him. Every man's port and bearing becomes somewhat more proud and lofty as he remembers that seventy-five years have rolled away, and that the great inheritance of Liberty is still his,— his, undiminished and unimpaired; his, in all its original glory; his to enjoy; his to protect; his to transmit to future generations.

THE FOURTH OF JULY

BY CHARLES LEONARD MOORE

(From *The Forum.*)

LET be the herds and what the harvest brings;
Give to oblivion all that's sold and bought,
The count of unrememberable things; —
Our better birthright is this day's report!
Live our sires in us?   Keep we their old skill
To know Occasion's whisper and be great?
Can our proud blood in one contagious thrill
Put admiration in the eyes of Fate?
Wide is our realm, and twin seas feel our yoke,
Aye, and the oarless ocean of the North; —
Are we then mightier than that scattered folk,
That fringe of clingers by the sea-beach froth
  Whose loins begat us?   Let to-morrow show
  If their stern arts hereditary grow.

LIFT UP YOUR HEARTS

ANONYMOUS

Sursum corda.   We have in our own time seen the
Republic survive an irrepressible conflict, sown in the
blood and marrow of the social order.   We have seen
the Federal Union, not too strongly put together in
the first place, come out of a great war of sections
stronger than when it went into it, its faith renewed,
its credit rehabilitated, and its flag saluted with love
and homage by sixty millions of God-fearing men
and women, thoroughly reconciled and homogeneous.
We have seen the Federal Constitution outlast the

strain, not merely of a Reconstructory ordeal and a
Presidential impeachment, but a disputed count of the
Electoral vote, a Congressional deadlock, and an extra constitutional tribunal, yet standing firm against
the assaults of its enemies, while yielding itself with
admirable flexibility to the needs of the country and
the time. And finally we saw the gigantic fabric of
the Federal Government transferred from the hands
that held it a quarter of a century to other hands, without a protest, although so close was the poll in the
final count that a single blanket might have covered
both contestants for the Chief Magisterial office.
With such a record behind us, who shall be afraid of
the future?

The young manhood of the country may take this
lesson from those of us who lived through times that
did indeed try men's souls — when, pressed down
from day to day by awful responsibilities and suspense, each night brought a terror with every thought
of the morrow, and when, look where we would, there
were light and hope nowhere — that God reigns and
wills, and that this fair land is and has always been
in His own keeping.

The curse of slavery is gone. It was a joint
heritage of woe, to be wiped out and expiated in
blood and flame. The mirage of the Confederacy has
vanished. It was essentially bucolic, a vision of Ar-
cadie, the dream of a most attractive economic fal-
lacy. The Constitution is no longer a rope of sand.
The exact relation of the States to the Federal Government, left open to double construction by the au-
thors of our organic being, because they could not
agree among themselves, and union was the para-
mount object, has been clearly and definitely fixed by

the three last amendments to the original chart, which constitute the real treaty of peace between the North and the South, and seal our bonds as a nation forever.

The Republic represents at last the letter and the spirit of the sublime Declaration. The fetters that bound her to the earth are burst asunder. The rags that degraded her beauty are cast aside. Like the enchanted princess in the legend, clad in spotless raiment and wearing a crown of living light, she steps in the perfection of her maturity upon the scene of this, the latest and proudest of her victories, to bid welcome to the world.

Need I pursue the theme? This vast assemblage speaks with a resonance and meaning which words can never reach. It speaks from the fields that are blessed by the never-failing waters of the Kennebec and from the farms that sprinkle the valley of the Connecticut with mimic principalities more potent and lasting than the real; it speaks in the whirr of the mills of Pennsylvania and in the ring of the woodcutter's axe from the forests of the lake peninsulas; it speaks from the great plantations of the South and West, teeming with staples that insure us wealth and power and stability, yea, from the mines and forests and quarries of Michigan and Wisconsin, of Alabama and Georgia, of Tennessee and Kentucky far away to the regions of silver and gold, that have linked the Colorado and the Rio Grande in close embrace, and annihilated time and space between the Atlantic and the Pacific; it speaks in one word, from the hearthstone in Iowa and Illinois, from the home in Mississippi and Arkansas, from the hearts of seventy millions of fearless, freeborn men and women, and that one word is "Union!"

There is no geography in American manhood. There are no sections to American fraternity. It needs but six weeks to change a Vermonter into a Texan, and there has never been a time, when, upon the battlefield, or the frontier, Puritan and Cavalier were not convertible terms, having in the beginning a common origin, and so diffused and diluted on American soil as no longer to possess a local habitation or a nativity, except in the National unit.

The men who planted the signals of American civilization upon that sacred Rock by Plymouth Bay were Englishmen, and so were the men who struck the coast a little lower down, calling their haven of rest after the great Republican commoner, and founding by Hampton Roads a race of heroes and statesmen, the mention of whose names brings a thrill to every heart. The South claims Lincoln, the immortal, for its own; the North has no right to reject Stonewall Jackson, the one typical Puritan soldier of the war, for its own! Nor will it! The time is coming, is almost here, when hanging above a mantel-board in fair New England — glorifying many a cottage in the sunny South — shall be seen bound together, in everlasting love and honor, two cross swords carried to battle respectively by the grandfather who wore the blue and the grandfather who wore the gray.

God bless our country's flag! and God be with us now and ever. God in the roof-tree's shade and God on the highway, God in the winds and waves, and God in our hearts!

ENGLAND AND THE FOURTH OF JULY

BY W. T. STEAD

(From *The Independent.*)

I WISH with all my heart that we could adopt the Fourth of July as the Festival Day of the whole English-speaking race. If this suggestion should seem strange to Americans, it is not unfamiliar to many Englishmen. We consider that the triumph of the American revolt against George III was a vindication of the essentially English idea of democratic self-government, and we believe that we have benefited by it almost as much as the Americans. It taught us a lesson which made the British Colonial Empire a possibility, and if we are now involved in a suicidal war in South Africa, it is largely because our Government has forgotten the principles of George Washington, and has gone back to the principles of George III.

For some years past I have presided at a distinctly British celebration of the Fourth of July at my brother's settlement in Southeast London, at Browning Hall, and I have always repudiated the idea that Americans should be allowed to monopolize the Fourth of July. It is one of the great days of the English-speaking race in the celebration of which all members of the English-speaking nations should participate.

SOME EARLY INDEPENDENCE DAY ADDRESSES

ADDRESS OF JOEL BARLOW (JULY 4, 1787)

(At Hartford, Conn.)

ON the anniversary of so great an event as the birth of the empire in which we live, none will question the propriety of passing a few moments in contemplating the various objects suggested to the mind by the important occasion; and while the nourishment, the growth, and even the existence of our empire depend upon the united efforts of an extensive and divided people, the duties of this day ascend from amusement and congratulation to a serious patriotic employment.

We are assembled, not to boast, but to realize, not to inflate our national vanity by a pompous relation of past achievements in the council or the field, but, from a modest retrospect of the truly dignified part already acted by our countrymen, from an accurate view of our present situation, and from an anticipation of the scenes that remain to be unfolded, to discern and familiarize the duties that still await us as citizens, as soldiers, and as men.

Revolutions in other countries have been affected by accident. The faculties of human reason and the rights of human nature have been the sport of chance and the prey of ambition. When indignation has burst the bands of slavery, to the destruction of one tyrant, it was only to impose the manacles of another. This arose from the imperfection of that early stage of society, the foundations of empires being laid in ignorance, with a total inability of foreseeing the improvements of civilization, or of adapting government to a state of social refinement. On the western continent a new task, totally unknown to the legislators of other nations, was imposed upon the fathers of the American empire. Here was a people, lords of the soil on which they trod, commanding a prodigious length of coast, and an equal breadth of frontier, a people habituated to liberty, professing a mild and benevolent religion, and highly advanced in science and civilization. To conduct such a people in a revolution, the address must be made to reason, as well as the passions.

In what other age or nation has a people, at ease upon their own farms, secure and distant from the approach of fleets and armies, tide-waiters and stamp-masters, reasoned, before they had felt, and, from the dictates of duty and conscience, encountered dangers, distress, and poverty, for the sake of securing to posterity a government of independence and peace? Here was no Cromwell to inflame the people with bigotry and zeal; no Cæsar to reward his followers with the spoils of vanquished foes; and no territory to be acquired by conquest. Ambition, superstition, and avarice, those universal torches of war, never illumined an American field of battle. But the permanent principles of sober policy spread through the colonies, roused the people to assert their rights, and conducted the revolution. Those principles were noble, as they were new and unprecedented in the history of human nations. The majority of a great people, on a subject which they understand, will never act wrong.

Our duty calls us to act worthy of the age and the

country that gave us birth. Every possible encouragement for great and generous exertions is presented before us. The natural resources are inconceivably various and great. The enterprising genius of the people promises a most rapid improvement in all the arts that embellish human nature. The blessings of a rational government will invite emigrations from the rest of the world and fill the empire with the worthiest and happiest of mankind; while the example of political wisdom and sagacity, here to be displayed, will excite emulation through the kingdoms of the earth, and meliorate the condition of the human race.

ADDRESS OF JOHN QUINCY ADAMS (JULY 4, 1793)

(At Boston.)

Americans! let us pause for a moment to consider the situation of our country at that eventful day when our national existence commenced. In the full possession and enjoyment of all those prerogatives for which you then dared to adventure upon "all the varieties of untried being," the calm and settled moderation of the mind is scarcely competent to conceive the tone of heroism to which the souls of freemen were exalted in that hour of perilous magnanimity.

Seventeen times has the sun, in the progress of his annual revolution, diffused his prolific radiance over the plains of independent America. Millions of hearts, which then palpitated with the rapturous glow of patriotism, have already been translated to brighter worlds; to the abodes of more than mortal freedom.

Other millions have arisen, to receive from their

parents and benefactors an inestimable recompense of their achievements.

A large proportion of the audience, whose benevolence is at this moment listening to the speaker of the day, like him, were at that period too little advanced beyond the threshold of life to partake of the divine enthusiasm which inspired the American bosom; which prompted her voice to proclaim defiance to the thunders of Britain; which consecrated the banners of her armies; and finally erected the holy temple of American Liberty over the tomb of departed tyranny.

It is from those who have already passed the meridian of life; it is from you, ye venerable assertors of the rights of mankind, that we are to be informed what were the feelings which swayed within your breasts and impelled you to action; when, like the stripling of Israel, with scarcely a weapon to attack, and without a shield for your defense, you met and, undismayed, engaged with the gigantic greatness of the British power.

Untutored in the disgraceful science of human butchery; destitute of the fatal materials which the ingenuity of man has combined to sharpen the scythe of death; unsupported by the arm of any friendly alliance, and unfortified against the powerful assaults of an unrelenting enemy, you did not hesitate at that moment, when your coasts were infested by a formidable fleet, when your territories were invaded by a numerous and veteran army, to pronounce the sentence of eternal separation from Britain, and to throw the gauntlet at a power, the terror of whose recent triumphs was almost coextensive with the earth.

The interested and selfish propensities which, in

times of prosperous tranquillity, have such powerful dominion over the heart, were all expelled, and in their stead the public virtues, the spirit of personal devotion to the common cause, a contempt of every danger, in comparison with the subserviency of the country, had assumed an unlimited control.

The passion for the public had absorbed all the rest, as the glorious luminary of heaven extinguishes, in a flood of refulgence, the twinkling splendor of every inferior planet. Those of you, my countrymen, who were actors in those interesting scenes will best know how feeble and impotent is the language of this description, to express the impassioned emotions of the soul with which you were then agitated.

Yet it were injustice to conclude from thence, or from the greater prevalence of private and personal motives in these days of calm serenity, that your sons have degenerated from the virtues of their fathers. Let it rather be a subject of pleasing reflection to you than the generous and disinterested energies which you were summoned to display, are permitted, by the bountiful indulgence of heaven, to remain latent in the bosoms of your children.

From the present prosperous appearance of our public affairs, we may admit a rational hope that our country will have no occasion to require of us those extraordinary and heroic exertions, which it was your fortune to exhibit.

But from the common versatility of all human destiny, should the prospect hereafter darken, and the clouds of public misfortune thicken to a tempest; should the voice of our country's calamity ever call us to her relief, we swear, by the precious memory of the sages who toiled and of the heroes who bled in her defense, that we will prove ourselves not unworthy of the prize which they so dearly purchased; that we will act as the faithful disciples of those who so magnanimously taught us the instructive lesson of republican virtue.

EXTRACT FROM ADDRESS OF JOHN LATHROP

(JULY 4, 1796)

(At Boston.)

In the war for independence America had but one object in view, for in independence are concentrated and condensed every blessing that makes life desirable, every right and privilege which can tend to the happiness, or secure the native dignity, of man. In the attainment of independence were all their passions, their desires, and their powers engaged. The intrepidity and magnanimity of their armies, the wisdom and inflexible firmness of their Congress, the ardency of their patriotism, their unrepining patience when assailed by dangers and perplexed with aggravated misfortune, have long and deservedly employed the pen of panegyric and the tongue of oratory.

Through the whole Revolutionary conflict a consistency and systematic regularity were preserved, equally honorable as extraordinary. The unity of design and classically correct arrangement of the series of incidents which completed the epic story of American independence, were so wonderful, so well wrought, that political Hypercriticism was abashed at the mighty production, and forced to join her sister, Envy, in applauding the glorious composition.

On the last page of Fate's eventful volume, with

the raptured ken of prophecy, I behold Columbia's name recorded, her future honors and happiness inscribed. In the same important book, the approaching end of tyranny and the triumph of right and justice are written, in indelible characters. The struggle will soon be over; the tottering thrones of despots will quickly fall, and bury their proud incumbents in their massy ruins.

THE FOURTH OF JULY

BY CHARLES SPRAGUE

To the sages who spoke, to the heroes who bled,
  To the day and the deed, strike the harp-strings of
    glory!
Let the song of the ransomed remember the dead,
  And the tongue of the eloquent hallow the story!
    O'er the bones of the bold
    Be the story long told,
  And on fame's golden tablets their triumphs
    enrolled
Who on freedom's green hills freedom's banner
  unfurled,
And the beacon-fire raised that gave light to the
  world!

They are gone — mighty men! — and they sleep in
    their fame:
  Shall we ever forget them? Oh, never! no, never!
Let our sons learn from us to embalm each great
    name,
  And the anthem send down —" Independence forever!"

Wake, wake, heart and tongue!
Keep the theme ever young;
Let their deeds through the long line of ages be sung
Who on freedom's green hills freedom's banner
unfurled,
And the beacon-fire raised that gave light to the
world!

OUR NATIONAL ANNIVERSARY

BY Ä. H. RICE

WE celebrate to-day no idle tradition — the deeds
of no fabulous race; for we tread in the scarcely obliterated footsteps of an earnest and valiant generation of men, who dared to stake life, and fortune,
and sacred honor, upon a declaration of rights, whose
promulgation shook tyrants on their thrones, gave
hope to fainting freedom, and reformed the political
ethics of the world.

The greatest heroes of former days have sought
renown in schemes of conquest, based on the love of
dominion or the thirst for war; and such had been
the worship of power in the minds of men, that adula-
tion had ever followed in the wake of victory. How
daring then the trial of an issue between a handful
of oppressed and outlawed colonists, basing their
cause, under God, upon an appeal to the justice of
mankind and their own few valiant arms. And how
immeasurably great was he, the fearless commander,
who, after the fortunes and triumph of battle were
over, scorned the thought of a regal throne in the
hearts of his countrymen. Amidst the rejoicings of
this day, let us mingle something of gratitude with

our joy — something of reverence with our gratitude — and something of duty with our reverence.

Let us cultivate personal independence in the spirit of loyalty to the State, and may God grant that we may always be able to maintain the sovereignty of the State in the spirit of integrity to the Union. Whatever shall be the fate of other governments, ours thus sustained, shall stand forever. As has been elsewhere said, nation after nation may rise and fall, kingdoms and empires crumble into ruin, but our own native land, gathering energy and strength from the lapse of time, shall go on and still go on its destined way to greatness and renown. And when thrones shall crumble into dust, when scepters and diadems shall have been forgotten, till heaven's last thunder shall shake the world below, the flag of the Republic shall still wave on, and its Stars, its Stripes, and its Eagle, shall still float in pride, and strength, and glory,

> " Whilst the earth bears a plant,
> Or the sea rolls a wave."

AMERICA'S NATAL DAY

BY JAMES GILLESPIE BLAINE

The United States is the only country with a known birthday. All the rest began, they know not when, and grew into power, they know not how. If there had been no Independence Day, England and America combined would not be so great as each actually is. There is no " Republican," no " Democrat," on the Fourth of July,— all are Americans. All feel that their country is greater than party.

CRISES OF NATIONS

BY DR. FOSS

THERE are brief crises in which the drift of individual and national history is determined, sometimes unexpectedly; critical moments on which great decisions hang; days which, like a mountain in a plain, lift themselves above the dead level of common days into everlasting eminence. Our Day of Independence was such a day; so was the day of Marathon, and the day of Waterloo. Napoleon admitted that the Austrians fought grandly on the field of Rivoli, and said, "They failed because they do not understand the value of minutes." Humboldt refers the discovery of America to "a wonderful concatenation of trivial circumstances," including a flight of parrots.

THE FOURTH OF JULY IN WESTMINSTER ABBEY

BY PHILLIPS BROOKS (JULY 4, 1880)

To all true men the birthday of a nation must always be a sacred thing. For in our modern thought the nation is the making-place of man. Not by the traditions of its history, nor by the splendor of its corporate achievements, nor by the abstract excellence of its Constitution, but by its fitness to make men, to beget and educate human character, to contribute to the complete humanity the perfect man that is to be,— by this alone each nation must be judged today. The nations are the golden candlesticks which

hold aloft the glory of the Lord. No candlestick can
be so rich or venerable that men shall honor it if it
hold no candle. " Show us your man," land cried to
land.

It is not for me to glorify to-night the country
which I love with all my heart and soul. I may not
ask your praise for anything admirable which the
United States has been or done. But on my country's birthday I may do something far more solemn
and more worthy of the hour. I may ask for your
prayers in her behalf: that on the manifold and
wondrous chance which God is giving her,— on her
freedom (for she is free, since the old stain of
slavery was washed out in blood); on her uncon-
strained religious life; on her passion for education
and her eager search for truth; on her zealous care for
the poor man's rights and opportunities; on her
quiet homes where the future generations of men are
growing; on her manufactories and her commerce; on
her wide gates open to the east and to the west; on her
strange meeting of the races out of which a new race
is slowly being born; on her vast enterprise and her
illimitable hopefulness,— on all these materials and
machineries of manhood, on all that the life of my
country must mean for humanity, I may ask you to
pray that the blessing of God, the Father of man, and
Christ, the Son of man, may rest forever.

III
BEFORE THE DAWN OF INDEPENDENCE

AMERICA RESENTS BRITISH DICTATION

BY HENRY B. CARRINGTON

(From *The Patriotic Reader*, J. B. Lippincott & Co., Phila.)

During the agitation of 1765, concerning the British Stamp Act, a convention of its opponents was assembled in New York City under the name of " The Stamp Act Congress." Among the most conspicuous of the delegates from the Massachusetts Colony was James Otis. As early as 1761 he protested so earnestly against permitting the British officers of the customs to have " writs of assistance " in their enforcement of the British revenue laws, that John Adams, who listened to his argument, thus described it:

" Otis was a flame of fire! With a promptitude of classical allusions, a depth of research, a rapid summary of historical events and dates, a profusion of legal authorities, a prophetic glance of his eye into futurity, and a rapid torrent of impetuous eloquence, he hurried away all before him. Every man of an immense audience appeared to me to go away, as I did, ready to take up arms against any ' writs of assistance.' "

The all-absorbing sentiment of his life, the wealth of his diction, and the fire of his oratory have been embodied in a form which stands among the best of American classics. In the romance of " The Rebels," Miss Lydia Maria Francis (afterwards Mrs. Child)

introduces James Otis as a leading character. After
the opening statement, that " there was hurrying to and
fro through the streets of Boston on the night of the
14th of August, 1765," his patriotic American woman
shows such a right conception of the power and oratory of Otis, as well as of the actual tone and spirit
of his times, that the fragments of her hero's conversation during the story, gathered in the form of a
speech, have often been mistaken for some actual
appeal to the people of his period. The youth of
America will do well to keep it fresh in mind, and
thereby honor both its author and its subject.

SPEECH OF JAMES OTIS IN 1765

ENGLAND may as well dam up the waters of the
Nile with bulrushes as to fetter the steps of Freedom,
more proud and firm in this youthful land than where
she treads the sequestered glens of Scotland or couches
herself among the magnificent mountains of Switzerland.   Arbitrary principles, like those against which
we now contend, have cost one king of England his
life, another his crown, and they may yet cost a third
his most flourishing colonies.

We are two millions, one-fifth fighting-men.   We
are bold and vigorous, and we call no man master.
To the nation from whom we are proud to derive our
origin we ever were, and we ever will be, ready to
yield unforced assistance; but it must not, and it never
can be extorted.

Some have sneeringly asked, Are the Americans
too poor to pay a few pounds on stamped paper?
No! America, thanks to God and herself, is rich.
But the right to take ten pounds implies the right to

take a thousand; and what must be the wealth that avarice, aided by power, cannot exhaust? True, the specter is now small; but the shadow he casts before him is huge enough to darken all this fair land. Others, in, sentimental style, talk of the immense debt of gratitude which we owe to England. And what is the amount of this debt? Why, truly, it is the same that the young lion owes to the dam which has brought it forth on the solitude of the mountain, or left it amid the winds and storms of the desert.

We plunged into the wave, with the great charter of freedom in our teeth, because the fagot and torch were behind us. We have waked this new world from its savage lethargy; forests have been prostrated in our path; towns and cities have grown up suddenly as the flowers of the tropics; and the fires in our autumnal woods are scarcely more rapid than the increase of our wealth and population.

And do we owe all this to the kind succor of the mother-country? No; we owe it to the tyranny that drove us from her; to the pelting storms which invigorated our helpless infancy!

But perhaps others will say, We ask no money from your gratitude; we only demand that you should pay your own expenses. And who, I pray, is to judge of their necessity? Why, the king! (And, with all due reverence to his sacred majesty, he understands the real wants of his distant subjects as little as he does the language of the Choctaws.) Who is to judge concerning the frequency of these demands? The ministry. Who is to judge whether the money is properly expended? The cabinet behind the throne.

In every instance, those who take are to judge for those who pay. If this system is suffered to go into operation, we shall have reason to esteem it a great privilege that rain and dew do not depend upon Parliament; otherwise, they would soon be taxed and dried.

But, thanks to God! There is freedom enough left upon earth to resist such monstrous injustice. The flame of liberty is extinguished in Greece and Rome, but the light of its glowing embers is still bright and strong on the shores of America. Actuated by its sacred influence, we will resist unto death.

But we will not countenance anarchy and misrule. The wrongs that a desperate community have heaped upon their enemies shall be amply and speedily repaired. Still, it is lighted in these colonies which one breath of their king may kindle into such fury that the blood of all England cannot extinguish it.

INDEPENDENCE A SOLEMN DUTY

BY RICHARD HENRY LEE

THE time will certainly come when the fated separation between the mother-country and these colonies must take place, whether you will or no, for it is so decreed by the very nature of things, by the progressive increase of our population, the fertility of our soil, the extent of our territory, the industry of our countrymen, and the immensity of the ocean which separates the two countries. And if this be true, as it is most true, who does not see that the sooner it takes place the better? — that it would be the height of folly not to seize the present occasion, when British injustice has filled all hearts with indignation, inspired all minds with courage, united all opinions in one, and put arms in every hand? And how long must we traverse three thousand miles of a stormy sea to solicit of arrogant and insolent men either counsel, or commands to regulate our domestic affairs? From what we have already achieved it is easy to presume what we shall hereafter accomplish. Experience is the source of sage counsels, and liberty is the mother of great men. Have you not seen the enemy driven from Lexington by citizens armed and assembled in one day? Already their most celebrated generals have yielded in Boston to the skill of ours. Already their seamen, repulsed from our coasts, wander over the ocean, the sport of tempests and the prey of famine. Let us hail the favorable omen, and fight, not for the sake of knowing on what terms we are to be the slaves of England, but to secure to ourselves a free existence, to found a just and independent government.

Why do we longer delay? why still deliberate? Let this most happy day give birth to the American Republic. Let her arise, not to devastate and conquer, but to reëstablish the reign of peace and the laws. The eyes of Europe are fixed upon us; she demands of us a living example of freedom that may contrast, by the felicity of her citizens, with the ever-increasing tyranny which desolates her polluted shores. She invites us to prepare an asylum where the unhappy may find solace and the persecuted repose. She entreats us to cultivate a propitious soil, where that generous plant which first sprang up and grew in England, but is now withered by the poisonous blasts of Scottish tyranny, may revive and flourish, sheltering under its salubrious and interminable shade all the unfortunate of the human race. This is the end presaged by so many omens;

by our first victories; by the present ardor and union; by the flight of Howe, and the pestilence which broke out among Dunmore's people; by the very winds which baffled the enemy's fleets and transports, and that terrible tempest which engulfed seven hundred vessels upon the coast of Newfoundland.

If we are not this day wanting in our duty to our country, the names of the American legislators will be placed, by posterity, at the side of those of Theseus, of Lycurgus, of Romulus, of Numa, of the three Williams of Nassau, and of all those whose memory has been and will be forever dear to virtuous men and good citizens.

AN APPEAL FOR AMERICA

BY WILLIAM PITT (LORD CHATHAM)

(In Parliament, January 20, 1775)

My Lords:

THESE papers, brought to your table at so late a period of this business, tell us what? Why, what all the world knew before: that the Americans, irritated by repeated injuries, and stripped of their inborn rights and dearest privileges, have resisted, and entered into associations for the preservation of their common liberties.

Had the early situation of the people of Boston been attended to, things would not have come to this. But the infant complaints of Boston were literally treated like the capricious squalls of a child, who, it is said, did not know whether it was aggrieved or not.

But full well I knew, at that time, that this child, if

not redressed, would soon assume the courage and voice of a man. Full well I knew that the sons of ancestors, born under the same free constitution and once breathing the same liberal air as Englishmen, would resist upon the same principles and on the same occasions.

What has government done? They have sent an armed force consisting of seventeen thousand men, to dragoon the Bostonians into what is called their duty; and, so far from once turning their eyes to the policy and destructive consequence of this scheme, are constantly sending out more troops. And we are told, in the language of menace, that if seventeen thousand men won't do, fifty thousand shall.

It is true, my lords, with this force they may ravage the country, waste and destroy as they march; but, in the progress of fifteen hundred miles, can they occupy the places they have passed? Will not a country which can produce three millions of people, wronged and insulted as they are, start up like hydras in every corner, and gather fresh strength from fresh opposition?

Nay, what dependence can you have upon the soldiery, the unhappy engines of your wrath? They are Englishmen, who must feel for the privileges of Englishmen. Do you think that these men can turn their arms against their brethren? Surely no. A victory must be to them a defeat, and carnage a sacrifice.

But it is not merely three millions of people, the produce of America, we have to contend with in this unnatural struggle; many more are on their side, dispersed over the face of this wide empire. Every Whig in this country and in Ireland is with them.

In this alarming crisis I come with this paper in my

hand to offer you the best of my experience and advice; which is, that a humble petition be presented to his Majesty, beseeching him that, in order to open the way toward a happy settlement of the dangerous troubles in America, it may graciously please him that immediate orders be given to General Gage for removing his Majesty's force from the town of Boston.

Such conduct will convince America that you mean to try her cause in the spirit of freedom and inquiry, and not in letters of blood.

There is no time to be lost. Every hour is big with danger. Perhaps, while I am now speaking, the decisive blow is struck which may involve millions in the consequence. And, believe me, the very first drop of blood which is shed will cause a wound which may never be healed.

When your lordships look at the papers transmitted to us from America, when you consider their firmness, decency, and wisdom, you cannot but respect their cause and wish to make it your own. For myself, I must affirm, declare, and avow that, in all my reading and observation (and it has been my favorite study, for I have read Thucydides, and have studied and admired the master-states of the world), I say, I must declare that, for solidity of reasoning, force of sagacity, and wisdom of conclusion, under such a complication of difficult circumstances, no nation or body of men can stand in preference to the General Congress at Philadelphia. I trust it is obvious to your lordships that all attempts to impose servitude upon such men, to establish despotism, over such a mighty continental nation, must be vain, must be fatal.

We shall be forced, ultimately, to retract. Let us retract while we can, not when we must. I say we must necessarily undo these violent, oppressive acts. They Must be repealed. You Will repeal them. I pledge myself for it that you will, in the end, repeal them. I stake my reputation on it. I will consent to be taken for an idiot if they are not finally repealed.

CONCILIATION OR WAR

EDMUND BURKE, IN PARLIAMENT, MARCH 22, 1775

WE are called again, as it were by a superior warning voice, to attend to America, and to review the subject with an unusual degree of calmness. Surely, it is an awful subject, or there is none this side the grave. The proposition is peace; not peace hunted through the medium of war, but peace sought in its natural course, in its ordinary haunts, and laid in principles purely pacific. I propose to restore the former unsuspecting confidence of the colonies in the mother-country, and reconcile them each to each. My hold of the colonies is in the close affection which grows from common names, from kindred blood, from similar privileges and equal protection. These are ties which, though light as air, are as strong as links of iron.

Let the colonies always keep the idea of their civil rights associated with your government; they will cling and grapple to you, and no force under heaven will be of power to tear them from their allegiance. But let it once be understood that your government may be one thing and their privileges another; that these two things may exist without any mutual relation; and the cement is gone, the cohesion is loosened, and everything hastens to decay and dissolution.

As long as you have the wisdom to keep the sovereign

authority of this country as the sanctuary of liberty, the sacred temple consecrated to our common faith, wherever the chosen race and sons of England worship freedom, they will turn their faces towards you. The more they multiply, the more friends you will have. The more ardently they love liberty, the more perfect will be their obedience.

Slavery they can have anywhere. It is a weed that grows in every soil. They may have it from Spain, they may have it from Prussia. But until you become lost to all feelings of your true interest and your national dignity, freedom they can have from none but you. This is the commodity of price, of which you have the monopoly.

This is the true Act of Navigation, which binds to you the commerce of the colonies, and through them secures to you the wealth of the world. Deny them this participation of freedom, and you break that sole bond which originally made, and must still preserve, the unity of the empire.

Do not entertain so weak an imagination as that your registers and your bonds, your affidavits and your sufferances, your cockets and your clearances, are what form the great securities of your commerce. Do not dream that your letters of office, and your instructions, and your suspending clauses, are the things that hold together the great contexture of this mysterious whole.

These things do not make your government, dead instruments, passive tools as they are; it is the spirit of the English constitution that gives all their life and efficacy to them. It is the spirit of the English constitution which, infused, through the mighty mass, pervades, feeds, unites, invigorates, vivifies every part of the empire, even down to the minutest member.

Is it not the same virtue which does everything for us here in England? Do you imagine, then, that it is the land tax which raises your revenue? that it is the annual vote in the committee of supply which gives you your army? or that it is the mutiny bill which inspires it with bravery and discipline?

No! surely no! It is the love of the people, it is their attachment to their government from the sense of the deep stake they have in such a glorious institution, which gives you your army and your navy, and infuses into both that liberal obedience without which your army would be a base rabble and your navy nothing but rotten timber.

All this, I know well enough, will sound wild and chimerical to the profane herd of those vulgar and mechanical politicians who have no place among us; a sort of people who think that nothing exists but what is gross and material, and who, therefore, far from being qualified to be directors of the great movement of empire, are not fit to turn a wheel in the machine.

But to men truly initiated and rightly taught, these ruling and master principles, which in the opinion of such men as I have mentioned have no substantial existence, are, in truth, everything and all in all. Magnanimity in politics is not seldom the truest wisdom, and a great empire and little minds go ill together. If we are conscious of our situation, and glow with zeal to fill our place as becomes our station and ourselves, we ought to auspicate all our public proceedings on America with the old warning of the church, *Sursum corda!* [1] We ought to elevate our minds to the greatness of that trust to which the order of Providence has called us.

By adverting to the dignity of this high calling, our ancestors have turned a savage wilderness into a glorious empire, and have made the most extensive and the only honorable conquests, not by destroying, but by promoting the wealth, the number, the happiness, of the human race.

"WAR IS ACTUALLY BEGUN"

BY PATRICK HENRY

(Mr. Henry in the Convention of Delegates of Virginia, March 23, 1775, urges that the colony be immediately put in a state of defense.)

THIS, sir, is no time for ceremony. The question before the house is one of awful moment to this country. For my own part, I consider it as nothing less than a question of freedom or slavery; and in proportion to the magnitude of the subject ought to be the freedom of the debate. It is only in this way that we can hope to arrive at truth, and fulfill the great responsibility which we hold to God and our country. Should I keep back my opinions at this time through fear of giving offense, I should consider myself as guilty of treason towards my country and of an act of disloyalty towards the majesty of Heaven, which I revere above all earthly kings.

Mr. President, it is natural to man to indulge in the illusions of hope. We are apt to shut our eyes against

[1] *Let your hearts rise upward!*

a painful truth, and listen to the song of that siren till she transforms us into beasts. Is this the part of wise men engaged in a great and arduous struggle for liberty? Are we disposed to be of the number of those who, having eyes, see not, and having ears, hear not, the things which so nearly concern their temporal salvation. For my part, whatever anguish of spirit it may cost, I am willing to know the whole truth; to know the worst, and to provide for it.

I have but one lamp by which my feet are guided, and that is the lamp of experience. I know of no way of judging of the future but by the past. And, judging by the past, I wish to know what there has been in the conduct of the British ministry for the last ten years to justify those hopes with which gentlemen have been pleased to solace themselves and the house? Is it that insidious smile with which our petition has been lately received? Trust it not, sir; it will prove a snare to your feet. Suffer not yourselves to be betrayed with a kiss. Ask yourself how this gracious reception of our petition comports with those warlike preparations which cover our waters and darken our land.

Are fleets and armies necessary to a work of love and reconciliation? Have we shown ourselves so unwilling to be reconciled that force must be called in to win back our love? Let us not deceive ourselves, sir. These are the implements of war and subjugation, the last arguments to which kings resort. I ask, sir, what means this martial array, if its purpose be not to force us to submission? Can the gentlemen assign any other possible motive for it? Has Great Britain any enemy in this quarter of the world, to call for all this accumulation of navies and armies? No, sir, she has none. They are meant for us; they can be meant for no other. They are sent over to bind and rivet upon us those chains which the British ministry have been so long forging.

And what have we to oppose them. Shall we try argument? Sir, we have been trying that for the last ten years. Have we anything new to offer upon the subject? Nothing. We have held the subject up in every light of which it is capable, but it has been all in vain. Shall we resort to entreaty and humble supplication? What terms shall we find which have not been already exhausted? Let us not, I beseech you, sir, deceive ourselves longer.

Sir, we have done everything that could be done to avert the storm that is now coming on. We have petitioned, we have remonstrated, we have supplicated, we have prostrated ourselves before the throne, and have implored its interposition to arrest the tyrannical hands of the ministry and Parliament. Our petitions have been slighted; our remonstrances have produced additional violence and insult; our supplications have been disregarded, and we have been spurned with contempt from the foot of the throne.

In vain, after these things, may we indulge the fond hope of peace and reconciliation. There is no longer any room for hope. If we wish to be free, if we mean to preserve inviolate those inestimable privileges for which we have been so long contending, if we mean not basely to abandon the noble struggle in which we have been so long engaged, and which we have pledged ourselves never to abandon until the glorious object of our contest shall be obtained, we must fight! I repeat it, sir, we must fight! An appeal to arms and to the God of hosts is all that is left us!

．　　．　　．　　．　　．　　．　　．　　．

They tell us, sir, that we are weak — unable to cope with so formidable an adversary. But when shall we be stronger? Will it be the next week, or the next year? Will it be when we are totally disarmed, and when a British guard shall be stationed in every house? Shall we gather strength by irresolution and inaction? Shall we acquire the means of effectual resistance by lying supinely on our backs, and hugging the delusive phantom of hope, until our enemies shall have bound us hand and foot? Sir, we are not weak if we make a proper use of those means which the God of nature hath placed in our power.

Three millions of people armed in the holy cause of liberty, and in such a country as that which we possess, are invincible by any force which our enemy can send against us. Besides, sir, we shall not fight our battles alone. There is a just God who presides over the destinies of nations, and who will raise up friends to fight our battles for us.

The battle, sir, is not to the strong alone; it is to the vigilant, the active, the brave. Besides, sir, we have no election. If we were base enough to desire it, it is now too late to retire from the contest. There is no retreat but in submission and slavery! Our chains are forged. Their clanking may be heard on the plains of Boston! The war is inevitable, and let it come! I repeat it, sir, let it come!

It is in vain, sir, to extenuate the matter. Gentlemen may cry peace, peace, but there is no peace. The war has actually begun! The next gale that sweeps from the north will bring to our ears the clash of resounding arms! Our brethren are already in the field! Why stand we here idle? What is it that the gentlemen wish? What would they have? Is life so dear, or peace so sweet, as to be purchased at the price of chains and slavery? Forbid it, Almighty God! I know not what course others may take, but as for me, *give me liberty or give me death!*

EMANCIPATION FROM BRITISH DEPENDENCE

BY PHILIP FRENEAU

(The following note in explanation of proper names, etc., in this poem is copied from Duyckinck's edition of Freneau.)

Note.— Sir James Wallace, Admiral Graves, and Captain Montague, were British naval officers, employed on our coast. The *Viper* and *Rose* were vessels in the service. Lord Dunmore, the last royal governor of Virginia, had recently in April, 1775, removed the public stores from Williamsburg, and, in conjunction with a party of adherents, supported by the naval force on the station, was making war on the province. William Tryon, the last Royal governor of New York, informed of a resolution of the Continental Congress: " That it be recommended to the several provincial assemblies in conventions and councils, or committees of safety, to arrest and secure every person in their respective colonies whose going at large may, in their opinion, endanger the safety of the colony or the liberties of America," discerning the signs of the times, took refuge on board the Halifax packet in the harbor, and left the city in the middle of October, 1775.

Libera nos, Domine — Deliver us, O Lord,
Not only from British dependence, but also,
From a junto that labor for absolute power,
Whose schemes disappointed have made them look
    sour;
From the lords of the council, who fight against free-
    dom
Who still follow on where delusion shall lead 'em.

From groups at St. James's who slight our Petitions,
And fools that are waiting for further submissions;
From a nation whose manners are rough and abrupt,
From scoundrels and rascals whom gold can corrupt.

From pirates sent out by command of the king
To murder and plunder, but never to swing;
From Wallace, and Graves, and *Vipers* and *Roses,*
Whom, if Heaven pleases, we'll give bloody noses.

From the valiant Dunmore, with his crew of banditti
Who plunder Virginians at Williamsburg city,
From hot-headed Montague, mighty to swear,
The little fat man with his pretty white hair.

From bishops in Britain, who butchers are grown,
From slaves that would die for a smile from the throne,
From assemblies that vote against Congress' proceed-
    ings,
(Who now see the fruit of their stupid misleadings).

From Tryon, the mighty, who flies from our city,
And swelled with importance, disdains the committee;
(But since he is pleased to proclaim us his foes,
What the devil care we where the devil he goes.)

From the caitiff, Lord North, who could bind us in
    chains,
From our noble King Log, with his toothful of brains,
Who dreams, and is certain (when taking a nap)
He has conquered our lands as they lay on his map.

From a kingdom that bullies, and hectors, and swears,
I send up to Heaven my wishes and prayers
That we, disunited, may freemen be still,
And Britain go on — to be damn'd if she will.

IV
THE DECLARATION

THE ORIGIN OF THE DECLARATION

BY SYDNEY GEORGE FISHER

BESIDES the semi-independent character of their political governments, there were other circumstances which tended to inspire a large part of the colonists with a strong passion for independence, and led them to resist with unusual energy the remodeling plans which England began in 1764.

The sturdy influences of Protestanism and American life had, however, not so great an effect on that large body of people called loyalists, whose numbers have been variously estimated at from one-third to over half the population. They remained loyal to England, and were so far from being inspired with a love of independence that they utterly detested the whole patriot cause and sacrificed their property and lives in the effort to stamp out its principles and put in their place the British empire method of alien control as the best form of government for America.

Patriot parties have existed in other countries without the aid of the particular influences which Burke described. The love of national independence is, in fact, the most difficult passion to eradicate, as the Irish, the Poles, and other broken nationalities bear witness. The desire for independence is natural to all

[1] *From " The Struggle for American Independence," by Sydney George Fisher, J. B. Lippincott & Co., Publishers, 1908.*

vigorous communities, is generally regarded as more manlike and honorable than dependence, and usually springs up spontaneously whether in Holland, Switzerland or America, in spite of the commercial and conservative influences of loyalism. But, nevertheless, the influences mentioned by Burke, and several that he did not mention, had no doubt considerable effect in creating the patriot party in America and inspiring it with enthusiasm and energy.

The self-confidence aroused in the colonists by their success in subduing the wilderness, felling the vast forests, hunting the wild game and still wilder red men, has often been given as a cause of the Revolution and the American love of independence. Eloquence is easily tempted to enlarge upon such causes, and to describe in romantic language the hunter and the woodsman, the farmer in the fresh soil of primeval forests, the fishermen of the Grand Banks, the merchants and sailors who traded with the whole world in defiance of the British navigation laws, and the crews of the whaling ships that pursued their dangerous game from the equator to the poles.

The American lawyers, according to Burke, were an important cause of the Revolution. They were very numerous in the colonies; law and theories of government were much read and studied, and the people were trained to discussion of political rights as well as of religious doctrine. Burke described in picturesque detail how, in the South, the ruling class lived scattered and remote from one another, maintaining themselves in self-reliant authority on plantations with hundreds of slaves; and slavery, he said, inspired in the white master a fierce love of independence for himself and an undying dread of any form of the bondage which his love of gain had inflicted on a weaker race.

The geographical position of the thirteen contiguous colonies, so situated that they could easily unite and act together, and having a population that was increasing so rapidly that it seemed likely in a few years to exceed the population of England, was possibly a more effective cause of the Revolution than any of those that have been named. The consciousness of possessing such a vast fertile continent, which within a few generations would support more than double the population of little England, furnished a profound encouragement for theories of independence. People in England were well aware of this feeling in the colonies, and Joshua Gee, a popular writer on political economy in 1738, tried to quiet their fears. Some, he said, were objecting that " if we encourage the Plantations they will grow rich and set up for themselves and cast off the English government " ; and he went on to show that this fear was groundless because the colonists nearly all lived on the navigable rivers and bays of America, where the British navy could easily reach and subdue them. He also attempted to argue away the advantage of the contiguous situation of the colonies and described them as split up into a dozen or more separate provinces, each with its own governor ; and it was inconceivable, he said, that such diverse communities would be able to unite against England.

English statesmen, however, saw the danger of union among the colonies long before the outbreak of the Revolution ; and they shrewdly rejected the plan of union of the Albany conference of 1754 ; and in the Revolution itself a large part of England's diplomatic and military efforts were directed towards breaking up the easy communication among the colonies.

In modern times England's colonies have been widely separated from one another. There has been no large and rapidly increasing white population on contiguous territory with ability for union. The dark-skinned population of India is enormous in numbers, but incapable of the united action of the Americans of 1776, and India is not considered a colony but a territory continuously held by overwhelming military force. Instead of a colonial population which threatened in a short time to outnumber her own people, England's power and population have, in modern times, grown far beyond any power or population in her well-scattered white colonies.

The colonists at the time of the Revolution have often been described as speaking of England as home and regarding the mother-country with no little degree of affection; and while there is no doubt some truth in this, especially as regards the people who were loyalists, yet a very large proportion of the colonists had become totally differentiated from the people of England. This was the inevitable result of having lived for over a hundred years in the American environment. They were no longer Englishmen. They had become completely Americanized. Certain classes kept up their connection with England, and many of the rich planters of the South sent their sons to England to be educated. But a very large part of the colonists, especially in the older settled provinces, like Massachusetts and Virginia, had forgotten England and were another people.

Instead of speaking, as novelists often describe them, in a formal archaic way, using quaint phrases of old English life, the colonists spoke with mannerisms and colloquial slang which were peculiarly American. These peculiarities were ridiculed by Englishmen of the time and formed part of Grant's famous speech in Parliament, the burden of which appears to have been that the colonists had become entirely different from English people, and Grant is said to have given imitations of what he considered their strange speech and manners. Mrs. Knight, in her *Journal of Travel from Boston to New York*, had, many years before the Revolution, given specimens of this difference; and the language of the New Englanders which she describes was certainly not like anything in England.

" Law for me — what in the world brings you here at this time of night? I never see a woman on the Rode so Dreadful late in all the days of my versall life. Who are you? Where are you going?" — Mrs. Knight's *Journal*, p. 23.

In 1775 some one wrote a set of humorous verses, said to have been the original Yankee Doodle song, to illustrate the colloquial Americanism of the time. " Slapping " was used for " large," as in the phrase " a slapping stallion." " Nation " was used for " a great deal," as in such a phrase as " only a nation louder." " Tarnal " was used for " very." " I see " was used for " I saw," " I come " for " I came," and " I hooked it off " in place of " I went away."

Not only did the patriots feel themselves to be quite different from Englishmen, but they had a consciousness of ability and power, the result of having governed themselves so long in their towns, counties, and provinces, and of having carried on a commerce of their own in defiance of the English navigation laws. They felt that they, not Englishmen, had created the country; and they had a resolute intention to develop its future greatness in their own way without the advice of aliens across three thousand miles of ocean.

This high confidence, which was a conspicuous motive in the patriot party, was always ridiculed by the loyalists as mere bumptiousness and conceit. It was difficult for a loyalist to understand how any one could seriously put himself in opposition to the British empire or want any form of government except the British constitution. But the patriot estimate of their own ability was by no means an exaggeration. They could be overcome, of course, as the Boer republics and other peoples have been overcome, by the superior numbers or wealth of Great Britain. But the history of the Revolution disclosed qualities in which the Americans notoriously excelled Europeans as well as the Anglo-Saxon stock in England from which they were derived. They were of keener practical intelligence, more promptness in action, more untiring energy, more originality in enterprise, better courage and endurance, and more natural military skill among the rank and file. These distinctively American qualities, we now call them, seem to have been much more in evidence among the patriot party than among the loyalists.

Every circumstance of their past and every consideration of their present convinced the patriot of the infinite pleasure and value of home rule and they had codified their opinions into a political philosophy which not only justified their semi-independence and disregard of acts of Parliament, but would also justify them in breaking off from England, at the first opportunity and becoming absolutely independent. They had gathered this philosophy from the works of certain European writers — Grotius, Puffendorf, Locke,

Burlamaqui, Beccaria, Montesquieu, and others —
who had applied to politics and government the doctrines of religious liberty and the right of private
judgment which had been developed by the Reformation. Being such extreme Protestants, and having carried so far the religious ideas of the Reformation, the
colonists naturally accepted in their fullest meaning the
political principles of the Reformation. If we are
looking for profound influences in the Revolution, it
would be difficult to find any that were stronger than
two of the writers just mentioned, Locke and Burlamaqui, whose books had a vast effect in the break-up
of the British empire which we are about to record.

Beginning with Grotius, who was born in 1582, and
ending with Montesquieu, who died in 1755, the writers
mentioned covered a period of about two hundred
years of political investigation, thought and experience.
In fact, they covered the period since the Reformation. They represented the effect of the Reformation
on political thought. They represented also all those
nations whose opinions on such subjects were worth
anything. Grotius was a Dutchman, Puffendorf a
German, Locke an Englishman, Burlamaqui an Italian
Swiss, and Montesquieu a Frenchman.

Hooker, who lived from 1553 to 1600, and whom
Locke cites so freely, might be included in the number,
and that would make the period quite two hundred
years. Hooker, in his " Ecclesiastical Polity," declared very emphatically that governments could not be
legitimate unless they rested on the consent of the
governed; and this principle forms the foundation of
Locke's famous essays.

There were, of course, other minor writers; and the
colonists relied upon them all; but seldom troubled

themselves to read the works of the earlier ones, or to read Hutchinson, Clarke and other followers of that school, because Locke, Burlamaqui, and Beccaria had summarized them all and brought them down to date. To this day any one going to the Philadelphia Library, and asking for No. 77, can take in his hands the identical, well-worn volume of Burlamaqui which delegates to the Congress and many an unsettled Philadelphian read with earnest, anxious minds. It was among the first books that the library had obtained; and perhaps the most important and effective book it has ever owned.

The rebellious colonists also read Locke's " Two Treatises on Government " with much profit and satisfaction to themselves. Locke was an extreme Whig, an English revolutionist of the school of 1688. Before that great event, he had been unendurable to the royalists, who were in power, and had been obliged to spend a large part of his time on the continent. In the preface of his " Two Treatises," he says that they will show how entirely legitimate is the title of William III to the throne, because it is established on the consent of the people. That is the burden of his whole argument — the consent of the people as the only true foundation of government. That principle sank so deep into the minds of the patriot colonists that it was the foundation of all their political thought, and became an essentially American idea.

Becarria, who, like Burlamaqui, was an Italian, also exercised great influence on the colonists. His famous book, " Crimes and Punishments," was also a short, concise, but very eloquent volume. It caused a great stir in the world. The translation circulated in America had added to it a characteristic commentary by Voltaire. Beccaria, though not writing directly on the subject of liberty, necessarily included that subject, because he dealt with the administration of the criminal law. His plea for more humane and just punishments, and for punishments more in proportion to the offense, found a ready sympathy among the Americans, who had already revolted in disgust from the brutality and extravagant cruelty of the English criminal code.

But Beccaria also stated most beautifully and clearly the essential principles of liberty. His foundation doctrine, that " every act of authority of one man over another for which there is not absolute necessity is tyrannical," made a most profound impression in America. He laid down also the principle that " in every human society there is an effort continually tending to confer on one part the highest power and happiness, and to reduce the other to the extreme of weakness and misery." That sentence became the life-long guide of many Americans. It became a constituent part of the minds of Jefferson and Hamilton. It can be seen as the foundation, the connecting strand, running all through the essays of the *Federalist*. It was the inspiration of the " checks and balances " in the national Constitution. It can be traced in American thought and legislation down to the present time.

Burlamaqui's book, devoted exclusively to the subject of liberty and independence, is still one of the best expositions of the true doctrines of natural law, or the rights of man. At the time of the Revolution these rights of man were often spoken of as our rights as men, which is a very descriptive phrase, because the essence of those rights is political manhood, honorable self-reliance as opposed to degenerate dependence.

Burlamaqui belonged to a Protestant family that had once lived at Lucca, Italy; but had been compelled, like the family of Turretini, and many others, to take refuge in Switzerland. He became a professor at Geneva, which gave him the reputation of a learned man. He also became a counselor of state and was noted for his practical sagacity. He had intended to write a great work in many volumes on the subject to which he had devoted so much of his life, " The Principles of Natural Law," as it was then called. Ill health preventing such a huge task, he prepared a single volume, which he said was only for beginners and students, because it dealt with the bare elements of the science in the simplest and plainest language.

This little book was translated into English in 1748, and contained only three hundred pages; but in that small space of large, clear type, Burlamaqui compressed everything that the patriot colonists wanted to know. He was remarkably clear and concise, and gave the Americans the qualities of the Italian mind at its best. He aroused them by his modern glowing thought and his enthusiasm for progress and liberty. His handy little volume was vastly more effective and far-reaching than would have been the blunderbuss he had intended to load to the muzzle.

If we examine the volumes of Burlamaqui's predecessors, Grotius, Puffendorf, and the others, we find their statements about natural law and our rights as men rather brief, vague, and general, as is usual with the old writers on any science. Burlamaqui brought them down to date, developed their principles, and swept in the results of all the thought and criticism since their day.

The term natural law, which all these writers used,

has long since gone out of fashion. They used it because, inspired by the Reformation, they were struggling to get away from the arbitrary system, the artificial scholasticism, the despotism of the middle ages. They were seeking to obtain for law and government a foundation which should grow out of the nature of things, the common facts of life that everybody understood. They sought a system that, being natural, would become established and eternal like nature; a system that would displace that thing of the middle ages which they detested, and called "arbitrary institution."

Let us, they said, contemplate for a time man as he is in himself, the natural man, his wants and requirements.

"The only way," said Burlamaqui, "to attain to the knowledge of that natural law is to consider attentively the nature and constitution of man, the relations he has to the beings that surround him, and the states from thence resulting. In fact, the very term of natural law and the notion we have given of it, show that the principles of this science must be taken from the very nature and constitution of man."

Men naturally, he said, draw together to form societies for mutual protection and advantage. Their natural state is a state of union and society, and these societies are merely for the common advantage of all of the members.

This was certainly a very simple proposition, but it had required centuries to bring men's minds back to it; and it was not altogether safe to put forth because it implied that each community existed for the benefit of itself, for the benefit of its members, and not for the benefit of a prince or another nation, or for the church, or for an empire.

It was a principle quickly seized upon by the Americans as soon as their difficulties began in 1764. In their early debates and discussions we hear a great deal about a " state of nature," which at first seems rather meaningless to us. But it was merely their attempt to apply to themselves the fundamental principles of the Reformation. Were the colonies by the exactions and remodeling of the mother-country thrown into that " state of nature," where they could reorganize society afresh, on the basis of their own advantage? How much severity or how much oppression or dissatisfaction would bring about this state of nature? Was there any positive rule by which you could decide? Patrick Henry, who was always very eloquent on the subject, declared that the boundary had been passed; that the colonies were in a state of nature.

Any one who is at all familiar with the trend of thought for the last hundred years can readily see how closely this idea of going back to natural causes and first conceptions for the discovery of political principles is allied to every kind of modern progress; to the modern study of natural history, the study of the plants and animals in their natural environment, instead of by preconceived scholastic theories; the study of the human body by dissection instead of by supposition; the study of heat, light, electricity, the soil, the rocks, the ocean, the stars by actual observation, without regard to what the Scriptures and learned commentators had to say.

A large part of the American colonists were very far advanced in all the ideas of the Reformation.

Burlamaqui's book, applying to politics and government, these free and wonderful principles, came to a large number of them as the most soul-stirring and mind-arousing message they had ever heard. It has all become trite enough to us; but to them it was fresh and marvelous. Their imaginations seized on it with the indomitable energy and passion which the climate inspired, and some who breathed the air of Virginia and Massachusetts were on fire with enthusiasm.

" This state of nature," argued Burlamaqui, " is not the work of man, but established by divine institution."

" Natural society is a state of equality and liberty; a state in which all men enjoy the same prerogatives, and an entire independence on any other power but God. For every man is naturally master of himself, and equal to his fellow-creatures so long as he does not subject himself to another person's authority by a particular convention."

Here we find coupled with liberty that word equality which played such a tremendous part in history for the succeeding hundred years. And we must bear in mind that what the people of that time meant by it was political equality, equality of rights, equality before the law and the government; and not equality of ability, talents, fortunes, or gifts, as some have fancied.

Burlamaqui not only found liberty, independence, and equality growing out of nature itself; but he argued that all this was part of the divine plan, the great order of nature and the universe. Indeed, that was what he and his Reformation predecessors had set out to discover, to unravel the system of humanity, to see if there really was a system that could be gathered from the actual plain facts; and to see also if there was a unity and completeness in this system.

"The human understanding," he says, "is naturally right, and has within itself a strength sufficient to arrive at the knowledge of truth, and to distinguish it from error." That he announces as the fundamental principle of his book, "the hinge whereon the whole system of humanity turns," and it was simply his way of restating the great doctrine of the Reformation, the right of private judgment.

But he goes on to enlarge on it in a way particularly pleasing to the patriot colonists, for he says we have this power to decide for ourselves, "especially in things wherein our respective duties are concerned."

"Yes," said the colonists, "we have often thought that we were the best judges of all our own affairs."

"Those who feel," said Franklin, in his examination before Parliament, "can best judge."

The daring Burlamaqui went on to show that liberty instead of being, as some supposed, a privilege to be graciously accorded, was in reality a universal right, inherent in the nature of things.

Then appears that idea common to the great leaders of thought in that age, that man's true purpose in the world is the pursuit of happiness. To this pursuit, they said, every human being has a complete right. It was part of liberty; a necessary consequence of liberty. This principle of the right to pursue happiness, which is merely another way of stating the right of self-development, has played as great a part in subsequent history as equality. It is one of the foundation principles of the Declaration of Independence. It is given there as the ground-work of the right of revolution, the right of a people to throw off or destroy a power which interferes with this great pursuit, " and to institute a new government, laying its foundation on such principles, and organizing its power in such form as to them shall seem most likely to effect their safety and happiness."

It has been interpreted in all sorts of ways — as the right to improve your condition, to develop your talents, to grow rich, or to rise into the class of society above you. It is now in its broadest meaning so axiomatic in this country that Americans can hardly realize that it was ever disputed.

But it was, and still is, disputed in England and on the continent. Even so liberal an Englishman as Kingsley resented with indignation the charge that he favored the aspiration of the lower classes to change their condition. Once a cobbler, remain a cobbler, and be content to be a good cobbler. In other words, the righteousness which he so loudly professed was intended to exalt certain fortunate individuals, and not to advance society.

This desire and pursuit of happiness being part of nature, or part of the system of Providence, and as essential to every man and as inseparable from him as his reason, it should be freely allowed him, and not repressed. This, Burlamaqui declares, is a great principle, "the key of the human system," opening to vast consequences for the world.

The consequences have certainly been vaster than he dreamed of. Millions of people now live their daily life in the sunshine of this doctrine. Millions have fled to us from Europe to seek its protection. Not only the whole American system of laws, but whole philosophies and codes of conduct have grown up under it. The abolitionists appealed to it, and freed six millions of slaves. The transcendental philosophy of New England, that extreme and beautiful attempt to develop conscience, nobility, and character from within; that call of the great writers like Lowell to every humble individual to stand by his own personality, fear it not, advance it by its own lines; even our education, the elective system of our colleges — all these things have followed under that "pursuit of happiness," which the patriot colonists seized upon so gladly in 1765 and enshrined in their Declaration of Independence in 1776.

They found in the principles of natural law how government, civil society, or "sovereignty," as those writers were apt to call it, was to be built up and regulated. Civil government did not destroy natural rights and the pursuit of happiness. On the contrary, it was intended to give those rights greater security and a fresh force and efficiency. That was the purpose men had in coming together to form a civil society for the benefit of all; that was the reason, as Burlamaqui put it, that "the sovereign became the depositary, as it were, of the will and strength of each individual."

This seemed very satisfactory to some of the colonists. You choose your sovereign, your government, for yourself, and make it your mere depositary or agent. Then as to the nature of the government, the right to govern, they were very much pleased to find that the only right there was of this sort was the right of each community to govern itself. Government by outside power was absolutely indefensible, because the notion that there was a divine right in one set of people to rule over others was exploded nonsense, and the assertion that mere might or superior power necessarily gave such right was equally indefensible. There remained only one plausible reason, and that was that superior excellence, wisdom, or ability might possibly give such right.

As to this " superior excellence " theory, if you admitted it you denied man's inherent right to liberty, equality and the pursuit of happiness; you denied his moral accountability and responsibility; you crippled his independent development, his self-development, his individual action; in a word, you destroyed the whole natural system.

Because a man is inferior to another is no reason why he should surrender his liberty, his accountability, his chance for self-development, to the superior. We do not surrender our property to the next man who is richer or an abler business manager. Our inferiority does not give him a right over us. On the contrary, the inferiority of the inferior man is an additional reason why he should cling to all those rights of nature which have been given to him, that he may have wherewithal to raise himself, and be alone accountable for himself. Or, as Burlamaqui briefly summarized it:

" The knowledge I have of the excellency of a superior does not alone afford me a motive sufficient to subject myself to him, and to induce me to abandon my own will in order to take his for my rule; . . . and without any reproach of conscience I may sincerely judge that the intelligent principle within me is sufficient to direct my conduct."

Only the people, Burlamaqui explained, have inherent inalienable rights; and they alone can confer the privilege of commanding. It had been supposed that the sovereign alone had rights, and the people only privileges. But here were Burlamaqui, Puffendorf, Montesquieu, Locke, and fully half the American colonists, undertaking to reverse this order and announcing that the people alone had rights, and the sovereign merely privileges.

These principles the Americans afterwards translated in their documents by the phrase, " a just government exists only by consent of the governed." All men being born politically equal, the colonies, as Dickinson and Hamilton explained, are equally with Great Britain entitled to happiness, equally entitled to govern themselves, equally entitled to freedom and independence.

It is curious to see the cautious way in which some of the colonists applied these doctrines by mixing them up with loyalty arguments. This is very noticeable in the pamphlets written by Alexander Hamilton. He gives the stock arguments for redress of grievances, freedom from internal taxation, government by the king alone, and will not admit that he is anything but a loyal subject. At the same time there runs through all he says an undercurrent of strong rebellion which leads to his ultimate object. " The power," he says, " which one society bestows upon any man or body of men can never extend beyond its own limits." This he lays down as a universal truth, independently of charters and the wonderful British Constitution. It applied to the whole world. Parliament was elected by the people of England, therefore it had no authority outside of the British isle. That British isle and America were separate societies.

" Nature," said Hamilton, " has distributed an equality of rights to every man." How then, he asked, can the English people have any rights over life, liberty, or property in America? They can have authority only among themselves in England. We are separated from Great Britain, Hamilton argued, not only by the ocean, by geography, but because we have no part or share in governing her. Therefore, as we have no share in governing her, she, by the law of nature, can have no share in governing us; she is a separate society.

The British, he said, were attempting to involve in the idea of a colony the idea of political slavery, and against that a man must fight with his life. To be controlled by the superior wisdom of another nation was ridiculous, unworthy of the consideration of manhood; and at this point he used that sentence which has so often been quoted —" Deplorable is the condition of that people who have nothing else than the wisdom and justice of another to depend upon."

Charters and documents, he declared, must yield to natural laws and our rights as men.

" The sacred rights of man are not to be rummaged for among old parchments or musty records. They are written as with a sunbeam in the whole volume of human nature by the hand of divinity itself and can never be erased by mortal power."

The Declaration of Independence was an epitome of these doctrines of natural law applied to the colonies. The Declaration of Independence originated in these doctrines, and not in the mind of Jefferson, as so many people have absurdly supposed. In order to see how directly the Declaration was an outcome of these teachings we have only to read its opening paragraphs:

" When, in the course of human events, it becomes

necessary for one people to dissolve the political bands which have connected them with another, and to assume, among the powers of the earth, the separate and equal station to which the laws of nature and of nature's God entitle them, a decent respect to the opinions of mankind requires that they should declare the causes which impel them to the separation.

" We hold these truths to be self-evident, that all men are created equal; that they are endowed by their Creator with certain inalienable rights; that among these are life, liberty and the pursuit of happiness. That, to secure these rights, governments are instituted among men, deriving their just powers from the consent of the governed; that, whenever any form of government becomes destructive of these ends, it is the right of the people to alter or to abolish it, and to institute a new government, laying its foundation on such principles, and organizing its powers in such form as to them shall seem most likely to effect their safety and happiness. Prudence, indeed, will dictate that governments long established should not be changed for light and transient causes; and, accordingly, all experience hath shown, that mankind are more disposed to suffer, while evils are sufferable, than to right themselves by abolishing the forms to which they are accustomed."

By understanding the writings of Burlamaqui, Locke, and Beccaria, which the colonists were studying so intently, we know the origin of the Declaration, and need not flounder in the dark, as so many have done, wondering where it came from, or how it was that Jefferson could have invented it. Being unwilling to take the trouble of examining carefully the influences which preceded the Declaration, historical students are sometimes surprised to find a document like the Virginia Bill of Rights or the supposed Mecklenburg resolutions, issued before the Declaration and yet containing the same principles. They instantly jump to the conclusion that here is the real origin and author of the Declaration, and from this Jefferson stole his ideas.

Jefferson merely drafted the Declaration. Neither he, Adams, Franklin, Sherman, nor Livingston, who composed the committee which was responsible for it, ever claimed any originality for its principles. They were merely stating principles which were already familiar to the people, which had been debated over and over again in Congress; which were so familiar in fact, that they stated them rather carelessly and took too much for granted. It would have been better, instead of saying, " all men are created equal," to have said that all men are created politically equal, which was what they meant, and what every one at that time understood. By leaving out the word " politically " they gave an opportunity to a generation unfamiliar with the doctrines of natural law to suppose that they meant that all men are created, or should be made, equal in conditions, opportunities or talents.

THE DECLARATION OF INDEPENDENCE

BY JOHN D. LONG

RECALL the quaint and homely city of Philadelphia, the gloom that hung over it from the terrible responsibility of the step there taken, the modest hall still standing and baptized as the Cradle of Liberty. On its tower swung the bell which yet survives with its legend,—" Proclaim liberty throughout all the world to all the inhabitants thereof." That day it rang out a proclamation of liberty that will indeed echo round the world and in the ears of all the inhabitants thereof long after the bell itself shall have crumbled into dust.

Hancock is in the president's chair; before him sit the half-hundred delegates who at that time represent America. Among the names it is remarkable how many there are that have since been famous in our annals. The committee appointed to draft the declarations are Jefferson, youngest and tallest; John Adams; Sherman, shoemaker; Franklin, printer; and Robert R. Livingston. If the patriot, Samuel Adams, at the sunrise of Lexington could say,—" Oh, what a glorious morning!" how well might he have renewed in the more brilliant noontime of July 4, 1776, the same prophetic words!

There is nothing in the prophecies of old more striking and impressive than the words of John Adams, who declared the event would be celebrated by succeeding generations as a great anniversary festival and commemorated as a day of deliverance, from one end of the continent to the other; that through all the gloom he could see the light; that the end was worth all the means and that posterity would triumph in the transaction. I am not of those who overrate the past. I know that the men of 1776 had the common weaknesses and shortcomings of humanity. I read the Declaration of Independence with no feeling of awe; and yet if I were called upon to select from the history of the world any crisis grander,

loftier, purer, more heroic, I should not know where
to turn.

It seems simple enough to-day, but it was something else in that day. The men who signed the
Declaration knew not but they were signing warrants
for their own ignominious execution on the gibbet.
The bloody victims of the Jacobite rebellions of 1715
and 1745 were still a warning to rebels; and the gory
holocaust of Culloden was fresh in the memory. But
it was not only the personal risk; it was risking the
homes, the commerce, the lives, the property, the
honor, the future destiny of three million innocent
people,— men, women, and children. It was defying
on behalf of a straggling chain of colonies clinging
to the sea-board, the most imperial power of the world.
It was, more than all, like Columbus sailing into
awful uncertainty of untried space, casting off from
an established and familiar form of government and
politics, drifting away to unknown methods, and upon
the dangerous and yawning chaos of democratic institutions, flying from ills they had to those they knew
not of, and perhaps laying the way for a miserable
and bloody catastrophe in anarchy and riot.

There are times when ordinary men are borne by
the tide of an occasion to crests of grandeur in conduct and action. Such a time, such an occasion, was
that of the Declaration. While the signers were
picked men, none the less true is it that their extraordinary fame is due not more to their merits than to
the crisis at which they were at the helm and to the
great popular instinct which they obeyed and expressed. And why do we commemorate with such
veneration and display this special epoch and event in
our history? Why do we repeat the words our

fathers spoke or wrote? Why cherish their names, when our civilization is better than theirs and when we have reached in science, art, education, religion, politics, in every phase of human development, even in morals, a higher level?

It is because we recognize that in their beginnings the eternal elements of truth and right and justice were conspicuous. To those eternal verities we pay our tribute, and not to their surroundings, except so far as we let the form stand for the spirit, the man for the idea, the event for the purpose. And it is also because we can do no better work than to perpetuate virtue in the citizen by keeping always fresh in the popular mind the great heroic deeds and times of our history. The valuable thing in the past is not the man or the events,— which are both always ordinary and which under the enchantment of distance and the pride of descent, we love to surround with exaggerated glory,— it is rather in the sentiment for which the man and the event stand. The ideal is alone substantial and alone survives.

THE SIGNING OF THE DECLARATION

BY GEORGE LIPPARD

IT is a cloudless summer day; a clear blue sky arches and expands above a quaint edifice rising among the giant trees in the center of a wide city. That edifice is built of plain red brick, with heavy window frames, and a massive hall door.

Such is the State House of Philadelphia in the year of our Lord 1776.

In yonder wooden steeple, which crowns the summit

of that red brick State House, stands an old man with snow-white hair and sunburnt face. He is clad in humble attire, yet his eye gleams as it is fixed on the ponderous outline of the bell suspended in the steeple there. By his side, gazing into his sunburnt face in wonder, stands a flaxen-haired boy, with laughing eyes of summer blue. The old man ponders for a moment upon the strange words written upon the bell, then, gathering the boy in his arms, he speaks: "Look here, my child; will you do this old man a kindness? Then hasten down the stairs, and wait in the hall below till a man gives you a message for me; when he gives you that word, run out into the street and shout it up to me. Do you mind?" The boy sprang from the old man's arms and threaded his way down the dark stairs.

Many minutes passed. The old bell-keeper was alone. "Ah!" groaned the old man, "he has forgotten me." As the word was upon his lips a merry, ringing laugh broke on his ear. And there, among the crowd on the pavement, stood the blue-eyed boy, clapping his tiny hands while the breeze blew his flaxen hair all about his face, and, swelling his little chest, he raised himself on tiptoe, and shouted the single word, "Ring!"

Do you see that old man's eye fire? Do you see that arm so suddenly bared to the shoulder? Do you see that withered hand grasping the iron tongue of the bell? That old man is young again. His veins are filling with a new life. Backward and forward, with sturdy strokes, he swings the tongue. The bell peals out; the crowds in the street hear it, and burst forth in one long shout. Old Delaware hears it, and gives it back on the cheers of her thousand sailors.

The city hears it, and starts up from desk and work-shop, as if an earthquake had spoken.

Under that very bell, pealing out at noonday, in an old hall, fifty-six traders, farmers and mechanics had assembled to break the shackles of the world. The committee, who had been out all night, are about to appear. At last the door opens, and they advance to the front. The parchment is laid on the table. Shall it be signed or not? Then ensues a high and stormy debate. Then the faint-hearted cringe in corners. Then Thomas Jefferson speaks his few bold words, and John Adams pours out his whole soul.

Still there is a doubt; and that pale-faced man, rising in one corner, speaks out something about " axes, scaffolds, and a gibbet." A tall, slender man rises, and his dark eye burns, while his words ring through the halls: " Gibbets! They may stretch our necks on every scaffold in the land. They may turn every rock into a gibbet, every tree into a gallows; and yet the words written on that parchment can never die. They may pour out our blood on a thou-sand altars, and yet, from every drop that dyes the axe, or drips on the sawdust of the block, a new martyr to freedom will spring into existence. What! are there shrinking hearts and faltering voices here, when the very dead upon our battle-fields arise and call upon us to sign that parchment, or be accursed forever?

" Sign! if the next moment the gibbet's rope is around your neck. Sign! if the next moment this hall rings with the echo of the falling axe. Sign! by all your hopes in life or death, as husbands, as fathers, as men! Sign your names to that parchment.

" Yes! were my soul trembling on the verge of

eternity; were this voice choking in the last struggle, I would still, with the last impulse of that soul, with the last gasp of that voice, implore you to remember this truth: God has given America to the free. Yes! as I sink down in the gloomy shadow of the grave, with my last breath I would beg of you sign that parchment."

SUPPOSED SPEECH OF JOHN ADAMS

BY DANIEL WEBSTER

SINK or swim, live or die, survive or perish, I give my hand and my heart to this vote. It is true, indeed, that in the beginning we aimed not at independence. But there is a Divinity which shapes our ends. The injustice of England has driven us to arms; and, blinded to her own interest and our good she has obstinately persisted, till independence is now within our grasp. We have but to reach forth to it, and it is ours. Why, then, should we defer the Declaration? Is any man so weak as now to hope for a reconciliation with England, which shall leave neither safety to the country and its liberties, nor safety to his life and his own honor? Are you not, sir, who sit in that chair, is not he, our venerable colleague near you, are you not both already the proscribed and predestined objects of punishment and of vengeance? Cut off from all hope of royal clemency, what are you, what can you be, while the power of England remains, but outlaws?

If we postpone independence, do we mean to carry on or give up the war? Do we mean to submit to the measures of Parliament, Boston Port-Bill and all?

Do we mean to submit, and consent that we ourselves shall be ground to powder, and our country and its rights trodden down in the dust? I know we do not mean to submit. We never shall submit. Do we mean to violate that most solemn obligation ever entered into by men, that plighting before God, of our sacred honor to Washington, when, putting him forth to incur the dangers of war, as well as the political hazards of the times, we promised to adhere to him, in every extremity, with our fortunes and our lives? I know there is not a man here, who would not rather see a general conflagration sweep over the land, or an earthquake sink it, than one jot or tittle of that plighted faith fall to the ground. For myself, having, twelve months ago, in this place, moved you, that George Washington be appointed commander of the forces raised, or to be raised, for defense of American liberty, may my right hand forget her cunning, and my tongue cleave to the roof of my mouth, if I hesitate or waver in the support I give him.

The war, then, must go on. We must fight it through. And if the war must go on, why put off longer the Declaration of Independence? That measure will strengthen us. It will give us character abroad. The nations will then treat with us, which they never can do while we acknowledge ourselves subjects in arms against our sovereign. Nay, I maintain that England herself will sooner treat for peace with us on the footing of independence than consent, by repealing her Acts, to acknowledge that her whole conduct toward us has been a course of injustice and oppression. Her pride will be less wounded by submitting to that course of things which now predestinates our independence than by yielding the points in controversy to her rebellious subjects. The former she would regard as the result of fortune; the latter she would feel as her own deep disgrace. Why, then, why, then, sir, do we not as soon as possible change this from a civil to a national war? And, since we must fight it through, why not put ourselves in a state to enjoy all the benefits of victory, if we gain the victory?

If we fail, it can be no worse for us. But we shall not fail. The cause will raise up armies; the cause will create navies. The people, the people, if we are true to them, will carry us, and will carry themselves, gloriously through the struggle. I care not how fickle other people have been found. I know the people of these Colonies, and I know that resistance to British aggression is deep and settled in their hearts, and cannot be eradicated. Every Colony, indeed, has expressed its willingness to follow, if we but take the lead.

Sir, the Declaration will inspire the people with increased courage. Instead of a long and bloody war for restoration of privileges, for redress of grievances, for chartered immunities, held under a British King, set before them the gloriousness of entire independence, and it will breathe into them anew the breath of life. Read this Declaration at the head of the army; every sword will be drawn from its scabbard, and the solemn vow uttered to maintain it, or to perish on the bed of honor. Publish it from the pulpit; religion will approve it, and the love of religious liberty will cling round it, resolved to stand with it, or fall with it. Send it to the public halls; proclaim it there; let them hear it who heard the first roar of the enemy's cannon; let them see it who saw their brothers and their sons fall on the field of Bunker Hill, and in the streets of Lexington and Concord, and the very walls will cry out in its support.

Sir, I know the uncertainty of human affairs, but I see, I see clearly, through this day's business. You and I, indeed, may rue it. We may not live to the time when this Declaration shall be made good. We may die; die, colonists; die, slaves; die, it may be, ignominiously and on the scaffold. Be it so; be it so! If it be the pleasure of heaven that my country shall require the poor offering of my life, the victim shall be ready at the appointed hour of sacrifice, come when that hour may. But, while I do live, let me have a country, or at least, the hope of a country, and that a free country.

But whatever may be our fate, be assured, be assured that this Declaration will stand. It may cost treasure, and it may cost blood, but it will stand, and it will richly compensate for both. Through the thick gloom of the present, I see the brightness of the future, as the sun in heaven. We shall make this a glorious, an immortal day. When we are in our graves, our children will honor it. They will celebrate it with thanksgiving, with festivity, with bonfires and illuminations. On its annual return, they will shed tears, copious, gushing tears, not of subjection and slavery, not of agony and distress, but of exultation, of gratitude and of joy. Sir, before God, I believe the hour is come. My judgment approves this measure, and my whole heart is in it. All that I have, and all that I am, and all that I hope, in this life, I am now ready here to stake upon it. And I leave off as I began, that, live or die, survive or perish, I am for the Dec-

laration. It is my living sentiment, and by the blessing of God it shall be my dying sentiment, Independence *now,* and INDEPENDENCE FOREVER!

THE LIBERTY BELL

BY J. T. HEADLEY

ON July fourth, 1776, the representatives of the
American people gathered at the State House in Philadelphia to take final action upon the Declaration of
Independence, which had been under discussion for
three days.

It was soon known throughout the city; and in the
morning, before Congress assembled, the streets were
filled with excited men, some gathered in groups engaged in eager discussion, and others moving toward
the State House. All business was forgotten in the
momentous crisis which the country had now reached.
No sooner had the members taken their seats than the
multitude gathered in a dense mass around the en-
trance. The bell-man mounted to the belfry, to be
ready to proclaim the joyful tidings of freedom as
soon as the final vote was passed. A bright-eyed boy
was stationed below to give the signal.

Around the bell, brought from England, had been
cast, more than twenty years before, the prophetic
motto: "Proclaim liberty throughout all the land,
unto all the inhabitants thereof." Although its loud
clang had often sounded over the city, the proclamation engraved on its iron lip had never yet been spoken
aloud.

It was expected that the final vote would be taken
without delay; but hour after hour wore on, and no

report came from the mysterious hall where the fate of a continent was in suspense. The multitude grew impatient. The old man leaned over the railing, straining his eyes downward, till his heart misgave him, and hope yielded to fear. But at length, about two o'clock the door of the hall opened, and a voice exclaimed, " It has passed!"

The word leaped like lightning from lip to lip, followed by huzzas that shook the building. The boy-sentinel turned to the belfry, clapped his hands, and shouted, "Ring! ring!" The desponding bell-man, electrified into life by the joyful news, seized the iron tongue and hurled it backward and forward with a clang that startled every heart in Philadelphia like a bugle blast.

"Clang! Clang!" the bell of Liberty resounded on, higher and clearer and more joyous, blending in its deep and thrilling vibration, and proclaiming in loud and long accents over all the land the motto that encircled it.

INDEPENDENCE BELL, PHILADELPHIA

INSCRIPTION, " PROCLAIM LIBERTY THROUGHOUT THE LAND TO ALL THE INHABITANTS THEREOF." JULY 4, 1776.

ANONYMOUS

THERE was tumult in the city,
   In the quaint Old Quaker town,
And the streets were rife with people
   Pacing restless up and down,—
People gathering at corners,
   Where they whispered each to each,

And the sweat stood on their temples
With the earnestness of speech.

As the bleak Atlantic currents
  Lash the wild Newfoundland shore,
So they beat against the State House,
  So they surged against the door;
And the mingling of their voices
  Made a harmony profound,
Till the quiet street of Chestnut
  Was all turbulent with sound.

" Will they do it? " " Dare they do it? "
  " Who is speaking? " " What's the news? "
" What of Adams? " " What of Sherman? "
  " Oh, God grant they won't refuse! "
" Make some way, there! " " Let me nearer! "
  " I am stifling! " " Stifle, then!
When a nation's life's at hazard,
  We've no time to think of men! "

So they beat against the portal,
  Man and woman, maid and child;
And the July sun in heaven
  On the scene looked down and smiled:
The same sun that saw the Spartan
  Shed his patriot blood in vain,
Now beheld the soul of freedom,
  All unconquered, rise again.

See! See! The dense crowd quivers
  Through all its lengthy line,
As the boy beside the portal
  Looks forth to give the sign!

With his little hands uplifted,
  Breezes dallying with his hair,
Hark! with deep, clear intonation,
  Breaks his young voice on the air.

Hushed the people's swelling murmur,
  List the boy's exultant cry!
"Ring!" he shouts, "Ring! Grandpa,
  Ring! oh, ring for Liberty!"
Quickly at the given signal
  The bell-man lifts his hand,
Forth he sends the good news, making
  Iron music through the land.

How they shouted! What rejoicing!
  How the old bell shook the air,
Till the clang of freedom ruffled
  The calmly gliding Delaware!
How the bonfires and the torches
  Lighted up the night's repose,
And from the flames, like fabled Phœnix,
  Our glorious Liberty arose!

That old State House bell is silent,
  Hushed is now its clamorous tongue;
But the spirit it awakened
  Still is living,— ever young;
And when we greet the smiling sunlight
  On the Fourth of each July,
We will ne'er forget the bell-man
  Who, betwixt the earth and sky,
Rung out, loudly, "INDEPENDENCE;"
  Which, please God, *shall never die!*

THE DECLARATION OF INDEPENDENCE

In Congress July 4, 1776

(The Unanimous Declaration of the Thirteen United States of America.)

WHEN in the course of human events, it becomes necessary for one people to dissolve the political bands which have connected them with another, and to assume, among the powers of the earth, the separate and equal station to which the laws of nature and of nature's God entitle them, a decent respect to the opinions of mankind requires that they should declare the causes which impel them to the separation.

We hold these truths to be self-evident, that all men are created equal, that they are endowed by their Creator with certain inalienable rights, that among these are life, liberty and the pursuit of happiness. That to secure these rights, governments are instituted among men, deriving their just powers from the consent of the governed, that, whenever any form of government becomes destructive of these ends, it is the right of the people to alter or to abolish it, and to institute a new government, laying its foundation on such principles and organizing its powers in such form, as to them shall seem most likely to effect their safety and happiness. Prudence, indeed, will dictate that governments long established should not be changed for light and transient causes; and, accordingly, all experience hath shown, that mankind are more disposed to suffer, while evils are sufferable, than to right themselves by abolishing the forms to which they are accustomed. But when a long train of abuses and usurpations, pursuing invariably the same object evinces a design to reduce them under absolute depotism, it is their right, it is their duty to throw off such government, and to provide new guards for their future security. Such has been the patient sufferance of these colonies; and such is now the necessity which constrains them to alter their former systems of government. The history of the present King of Great Britain is a history of repeated injuries and usurpations, all having, in direct object, the establishment of an absolute tyranny over these states. To prove this, let facts be submitted to a candid world: —

He has refused his assent to laws, the most wholesome and necessary for the public good.

He has forbidden his Governors to pass laws of immediate and pressing importance, unless suspended in their operation till his assent should be obtained; and when so suspended, he has utterly neglected to attend to them.

He has refused to pass other laws for the accommodation of large districts of people, unless those people would relinquish the right of representation in the legislature; a right inestimable to them, and formidable to tyrants only.

He has called together legislative bodies at places unusual, uncomfortable, and distant from the depository of their public records, for the sole purpose of fatiguing them into compliance with his measures.

He has dissolved representative houses repeatedly, for opposing with manly firmness his invasions on the rights of the people.

He has refused for a long time, after such dissolutions, to cause others to be elected; whereby the legislative powers, incapable of annihilation, have returned to the people at large for their exercise; the State remaining in the meantime exposed to all the dangers of invasion from without, and convulsions within.

He has endeavored to prevent the population of these States; for that purpose obstructing the laws for naturalization of foreigners; refusing to pass others to encourage their migration hither, and raising the conditions of new appropriations of lands.

He has obstructed the administration of justice, by refusing his assent to laws for establishing judiciary powers.

He has made judges dependent on his will alone, for the tenure of their offices, and the amount and payment of their salaries.

He has erected a multitude of new offices, and sent hither swarms of officers to harass our people, and eat out their substance.

He has kept among us, in times of peace, standing armies without the consent of our legislature.

He has affected to render the military independent of, and superior to, the civil power.

He has combined, with others, to subject us to a jurisdiction foreign to our constitution, and unacknowledged by our laws; giving his assent to their acts of pretended legislation:

For quartering large bodies of armed troops among us:

For protecting them, by a mock trial, from punishment for any murders which they should commit on the inhabitants of these States:

For cutting off our trade with all parts of the world:

For imposing taxes on us without our consent:

For depriving us in many cases, of the benefits of trial by jury:

For transporting us beyond seas to be tried for pretended offenses:

For abolishing the free system of English laws in a neighboring province, establishing therein an arbitrary government, and enlarging its boundaries so as to render it at once an example and fit instrument for introducing the same absolute rule into these colonies:

For taking away our charters, abolishing our most valuable laws, and altering, fundamentally, the powers of our governments:

For suspending our own legislatures, and declaring themselves invested with power to legislate for us in all cases whatsoever.

He has abdicated government here, by declaring us out of his protection and waging war against us.

He has plundered our seas, ravaged our coasts, burnt our towns, and destroyed the lives of our people.

He is, at this time, transporting large armies of foreign mercenaries to complete the works of death, desolation and tyranny, already begun with circumstances of cruelty and perfidy scarcely paralleled in the most barbarous ages, and totally unworthy the head of a civilized nation.

He has constrained our fellow citizens, taken captive on the high seas, to bear arms against their country, to become the executioners of their friends and brethren, or to fall themselves by their hands.

He has excited domestic insurrections amongst us, and has endeavored to bring on the inhabitants of our frontiers, the merciless Indian savages, whose known rule of warfare is an undistinguished destruction of all ages, sexes and conditions.

In every stage of these oppressions we have petitioned for redress in the most humble terms; our repeated petitions have been answered only by repeated injury. A prince, whose character is thus marked by every act which may define a tyrant, is unfit to be the ruler of a free people.

Nor have we been wanting in attention to our British brethren. We have warned them from time to time of attempts made by their legislature to extend an unwarrantable jurisdiction over us. We have reminded them of the circumstances of our emigration and settlement here. We have appealed to their native justice and magnanimity, and we have conjured them, by the ties of our common kindred, to disavow these usurpations, which would inevitably interrupt our connections and correspondence. They, too, have been deaf to the voice of justice and consanguinity. We must, therefore, acquiesce in the necessity, which denounces our separation, and hold them, as we hold the rest of mankind, enemies in war, in peace, friends.

We, therefore, the representatives of the United States of America, in General Congress assembled, appealing to the Supreme Judge of the World for the rectitude of our intentions, do, in the name, and by the authority of the good people of these colonies, solemnly publish and declare, That these United Colonies are, and of right ought to be, Free and Independent States; that they are absolved from all allegiance to the British crown, and that all political connection between them and the state of Great Britain is, and ought to be, totally dissolved; and that, as Free and Independent States, they have full power to levy war, conclude peace, contract alliances, establish commerce, and to do all other acts and things which Independent States may of right do. And, for the support of this declaration, with a firm reliance on the protection of

Divine Providence, we mutually pledge to each other, our lives, our fortunes, and our sacred honor.

JOHN HANCOCK

(New Hampshire) JOSIAH BARTLETT, WM. WHIPPLE, MATTHEW THORNTON.

(Massachusetts Bay) SAML. ADAMS, JOHN ADAMS, ROBT. TREAT PAINE, ELBRIDGE GERRY.

(Rhode Island) STEP. HOPKINS, WILLIAM ELLERY.

(Connecticut) ROGER SHERMAN, SAM'EL HUNTINGTON, WM. WILLIAMS, OLIVER WOLCOTT.

(New York) WM. FLOYD, PHIL. LIVINGSTON, FRANC. LEWIS, LEWIS MORRIS.

(New Jersey) RICHD. STOCKTON, JNO. WITHERSPOON, FRANS. HOPKINSON, JOHN HART, ABRA. CLARK.

(Pennsylvania) ROBT. MORRIS, BENJAMIN RUSH, BENJ. FRANKLIN, JOHN MORTON, GEO. CLYMER, JAS. SMITH, GEO. TAYLOR, JAMES WILSON, GEO. ROSS.

(Delaware) CÆSAR · RODNEY, GEO. REED, THO. M'KEAN.

(Maryland) SAMUEL CHASE, WM. PACA, THOS. STONE, CHARLES CARROLL of Carrollton.

(Virginia) GEORGE WYTHE, RICHARD HENRY LEE, TH. JEFFERSON, BENJA. HARRISON, THOS. NELSON, JR., FRANCIS LIGHTFOOT LEE, CARTER BRAXTON.

(North Carolina) WM. HOOPER, JOSEPH HEWES, JOHN PENN.

(South Carolina) EDWARD RUTLEDGE, THOS. HEYWARD, JUNR., THOMAS LYNCH, JUNR., ARTHUR MIDDLETON.

(Georgia) BUTTON GWINNETT, LYMAN HALL, GEO. WALTON.

INDEPENDENCE EXPLAINED

BY SAMUEL ADAMS

(Delivered in Philadelphia, August 1, 1776, twenty-seven days after the Declaration of Independence.)

My countrymen, from the day on which an accommodation takes place between England and America on any other terms than as independent States, I shall date the ruin of this country. We are now, to the astonishment of the world, three millions of souls united in one common cause. This day we are called on to give a glorious example of which the wisest and best of men were rejoiced to view only in speculation. This day presents the world with the most august spectacle that its annals ever unfolded,— millions of freemen voluntarily and deliberately forming themselves into a society for their common defense and common happiness. Immortal spirits of Hampden, Locke, and Sidney! will it not add to your benevolent joys to behold your posterity rising to the dignity of *men* — evincing to the world the reality and expediency of your systems, and in the actual enjoyment of that equal liberty which you were happy when on earth in delineating and recommending to mankind?

Other nations have received their laws from conquerors; some are indebted for a constitution to the sufferings of their ancestors through revolving centuries; the people of this country alone have formally and deliberately chosen a government for themselves, and, with open, uninfluenced consent, bound themselves into a social compact. And, fellow countrymen, if ever it was granted to mortals to trace the designs of Providence and interpret its manifestations in favor of their cause, we may, with humility of soul, cry out, NOT UNTO US, NOT UNTO US, BUT TO THY NAME BE THE PRAISE. The confusion of the devices of our enemies, and the rage of the elements against them, have done almost as much towards our success as either our counsels or our arms.

The time at which this attempt in our liberties was made,— when we were ripened into maturity, had acquired a knowledge of war, and were free from the incursions of intestine enemies,— the *gradual* advances of our oppressors, enabling us to prepare for our defense, the unusual fertility of our lands, the clemency of the seasons, the success which at first attended our feeble arms, producing unanimity among our friends and compelling our internal foes to acquiescence,— these are all strong and palpable marks and assurances that Providence IS YET GRACIOUS UNTO ZION, THAT IT WILL TURN AWAY THE CAPTIV-ITY OF JACOB! Driven from every other corner of the earth, freedom of thought and the right of private judgment in matters of conscience direct their course to this happy country as their last asylum. Let us cherish the noble guests! Let us shelter them under the wings of universal toleration! Be this the seat of UNBOUNDED RELIGIOUS FREEDOM! She will bring with her in her train, Industry, Wisdom, and Commerce.

Our union is now complete. You have in the first armies sufficient to repel the whole force of your enemies. The hearts of your soldiers beat high with the spirit of freedom. Go on, then, in your generous enterprise, with gratitude to heaven for past success, and confidence of it in the future! For my own part, I ask no greater blessing than to share with you the common danger and the common glory. If I have a wish dearer to my soul than that my ashes may be mingled with those of a Warren and a Montgomery, it is, THAT THESE AMERICAN STATES MAY NEVER CEASE TO BE FREE AND INDEPENDENT!

THE DIGNITY OF OUR NATION'S FOUNDERS

BY WILLIAM M. EVARTS

THE Declaration of Independence was, when it occurred, a capital transaction in human affairs; as such it has kept its place in history; as such it will maintain itself while human interest in human institutions shall endure. The scene and the actors, for their profound impression on the world, at the time and ever since, have owed nothing to dramatic effects, nothing to epical exaggerations. To the eye there was nothing wonderful or vast or splendid or pathetic in the movement or the display. Imagination or art can give no sensible grace or decoration to the persons, the place, or the performance which made up the business of that day. The worth and force that belong to the agents and the action rest wholly on the wisdom, the courage and the faith that formed and executed the great design, and the potency and permanence of its operation upon the affairs of the world which followed as foreseen and legitimate consequences.

The dignity of the act is the deliberate, circumspect, open and serene performance by these men, in the clear light of day and by a concurrent purpose, of a civic duty which embraced the greatest hazards to themselves and to all the people from whom they held this disputed discretion but which to their sober judgments promised benefits to that people and to their posterity, exceeding these hazards and commensurate with its own fitness. The question of their conduct is to be measured by the actual weight and pressure of the manifold considerations which surrounded the subject before them and by the abundant evidence that they comprehended their vastness and variety. By a voluntary and responsible choice they willed to do what was done and what without their will would not have been done.

Thus estimated, the illustrious act covers all who participated in it with its own renown and makes them forever conspicuous among men, as it is forever famous among events. And thus the signers of our Declaration of Independence "wrote their names where all nations should behold them and all time should not efface them." It was " in the course of human events " intrusted to them to determine whether the fullness of time had come when a nation should be born in a day. They declared the independence of a new nation in the sense in which men declare emancipation or declare war,— the declaration created what was declared.

Famous always among men are the founders of states and fortunate above all others in such fame are these, our fathers, whose combined wisdom and courage began the great structure of our national existence and laid sure the foundations of liberty and justice on which it rests. Fortunate first in the clearness of their title and in the world's acceptance of their rightful claim. Fortunate next in the enduring magnitude of the State they founded and the beneficence of its protection of the vast interests of human life and happiness which have here had their home. Fortunate again in the admiring imitations of their work which the institutions of the most powerful and most advanced nations more and more exhibit. Fortunate last of all in the full demonstration of our later time that their work is adequate to withstand the most disastrous storms of human fortunes and survive unwrecked, unshaken and unharmed.

THE CHARACTER OF THE DECLARATION OF INDEPENDENCE

BY GEORGE BANCROFT

THIS immortal State paper, which for its composer was the aurora of enduring fame, was " the genuine effusion of the soul of the country at that time," the revelation of its mind, when, in its youth, its enthusiasm, its sublime confronting of danger, it rose to the highest creative powers of which man is capable. The bill of rights which it promulgates is of rights that are older than human institutions, and spring from the eternal justice that is anterior to the State.

Two political theories divided the world: one founded the Commonwealth on the reason of State, the policy of expediency; the other on the immutable principles of morals. The new Republic, as it took its place among the powers of the world, proclaimed its faith in the truth and reality and unchangeableness of freedom, virtue and right.

The heart of Jefferson, in writing the Declaration, and of Congress in adopting it, beat for all humanity; the assertion of right was made for the entire world of mankind, and all coming generations, without any exception whatever; for the proposition which admits of exceptions can never be self-evident. As it was put forth in the name of the ascendant people of that time, it was sure to make the circuit of the world, passing everywhere through the despotic countries of Europe; and the astonished nations, as they read that all men are created equal, started out of their lethargy, like those who have been exiles from childhood, when they suddenly hear the dimly remembered accents of their mother tongue.

THE DECLARATION OF INDEPENDENCE

BY HENRY T. RANDALL

To the Patriots, the Declaration gave strength and courage. It gave them a definite purpose,— and a name and object commensurate with the cost. When it was formally read by the magistracy from the halls of justice and in the public marts by the officers of the army at the head of their divisions, by the clergy from their pulpits, its grandeur impressed the popular imagination. The American people pronounced it a fit instrument, clothed in fitting words. The public enthusiasm burst forth, sometimes in gay and festive, and sometimes in solemn and religious, observances — as the Cavalier or Puritan taste predominated.

In the Southern and Middle cities and villages, the riotous populace tore down the images of monarchs and Colonial governors and dragged them with ropes round their necks through the streets — cannon thundered, bonfires blazed — the opulent feasted, drank toasts, and joined in hilarious celebrations. In New

England, the grimmer joy manifested itself in prayers and sermons, and in religious rites.

THE DECLARATION OF INDEPENDENCE

BY JOHN QUINCY ADAMS

THE Declaration of Independence! The interest which in that paper has survived the occasion upon which it was issued; the interest which is of every age and every clime; the interest which quickens with the lapse of years, spreads as it grows old, and brightens as it recedes, is in the principles which it proclaims. It was the first solemn declaration, by a nation, of the only legitimate foundation of civil government. It was the corner stone of a new fabric, destined to cover the surface of the globe. It demolished at a stroke the lawfulness of all governments founded upon conquest. It swept away all the rubbish of accumulated centuries of servitude. It announced in practical form to the world the transcendent truth of the inalienable sovereignty of the people. It proved that the social compact was no figment of the imagination, but a real, solid, and sacred bond of the social union. From the day of this declaration the people of North America were no longer the fragment of a distant empire, imploring justice and mercy from an inexorable master in another hemisphere. They were no longer children, appealing in vain to the sympathies of a heartless mother; no longer subjects, leaning upon the shattered columns of royal promises, and invoking the faith of parchment to secure their rights. They were a nation, asserting

as of right, and maintaining by war, its own existence.
A nation was born in a day.

> " How many ages hence
> Shall this, their lofty scene, be acted o'er
> In states unborn, and accents yet unknown? "

It will be acted o'er, but it never can be repeated.
It stands, and must forever stand, alone; a beacon
on the summit of the mountain, to which all the inhabitants of the earth may turn their eyes for a genial
and saving light, till time shall be lost in eternity, and
this globe itself dissolves, nor leave a wreck behind.
It stands forever, a light of admonition to the rulers of
men, a light of salvation and redemption to the oppressed. So long as this planet shall be inhabited by
human beings, so long as man shall be of social nature,
so long as government shall be necessary to the great
moral purposes of society, so long as it shall be abused
to the purposes of oppression — so long shall this
Declaration hold out to the sovereign and to the subject the extent and boundaries of their respective
rights and duties, founded in the laws of nature and of
nature's God.

THE DECLARATION OF INDEPENDENCE [1]

BY TUDOR JENKS

" WHAT is the most dramatic incident in American
history and why? "

The emphatic and determining word in this ques-

[1] *From " The Chautauquan," 1900.*

tion is the adverb "most." To answer conclusively, the method must be comparative; it is not enough to stir the emotions of patriotism, to excite the imagination of the poetic soul, to depict with skill bygone scenes so that they live again. The intellectual faculties must be satisfied that the chosen incident is truly an incident, that it is dramatic, and that it is more dramatic than all others in our history.

Definition seems but a poor prelude to the drama, but as the defender of the Constitution began his reply to Hayne by asking for the reading of the resolution before the Senate, it may be permissible to refer to the dictionary for guidance, as the storm-tossed mariner of Webster's metaphor glanced at the sun to rectify his course.

"Incident," as used in the given question, can mean only "something which takes place in connection with an event or series of events of greater importance" (Century Dictionary), since any broader meaning of the word would be too inclusive, and might permit the naming of a whole epoch.

"Dramatic" (by the same author) is "characterized by the force and animation in act or expression appropriate to the drama." Force and animation may of course be psychical or physical; but if psychical they must find expression in some form appreciable by the senses, else they are not dramatic.

Bearing these guiding principles in mind, let us see in what moment of American history we shall find that incident so connected with greater events, and so expressed as to be "The most dramatic"—that incident toward which all preceding events led, and from which subsequent events have sprung. Let us then select as expressing that incident the most forceful and animated action that would be appropriate to dramatic representation.

The periods of American history are the traditionary, that of discovery and exploration, that of colonization. These three are preparatory, and "American" only in a geographical sense. Then come the period of revolution, that of nationality and rebellion and finally the present — which may be called the period of expansion, since it marks for good or for evil the birth of the nation as a world power.

These periods group naturally into two great classes: I. America as an appanage of Europe. II. America as independent. The transition from one existence to the other took place in an instant of time. Before the Declaration of Independence our nation did not exist; once that document was ratified, the United States was created a nation.

Here, then, is the dividing of the ways; here the act of divine creation of which our forefathers were but the human instruments. This is the one universally celebrated and commemorated moment in our history — the birth of "a new nation conceived in liberty, and dedicated to the proposition that all men are created equal."

The great Civil war was but the test whether that nation could endure; so said Lincoln, whom we are learning to know as our greatest statesman. All our subsequent history is but the voyage of the ship of state by the chart then drafted.

Toward the Declaration converge all previous lines of historical development; from the Declaration diverge all the lines along which patriotic statesmanship must hereafter guide the national future. Deviations from these converging and diverging paths have been but blind trails to be painfully retraced.

Here, then, let us repeat, is the focus of our national life.

In what act, in what incident shall we find this moment of time expressed most dramatically?

The streets of Philadelphia were thronged with citizens awaiting news of the action of Congress. Within the old State House were the councilors of the colonies — the group of contemporaries whom Gladstone declared unequaled in the history of the world. One by one the names of the representatives were signed to that document which was to commit them to death as rebels or to immortality as patriots.

As the last name was affixed, a little boy ran from the doorway out into the street, and, tossing his arms above his head, gave forth the tidings of a nation's birth in the words:

"Ring! *Ring!* RING!"

and then the Liberty Bell echoed the gospel, as foreordained in its inscription: " Proclaim liberty to the land: to all the inhabitants thereof."

That is the most dramatic incident in American history.

Whether we view its inception or its outcome, it stands unrivaled. We shall forever " celebrate it with thanksgiving " so long as the nation endures.

This incident responds to every test. It is the action of a single person actuated by intense emotion; he, a child, was a type of the fact he expressed; through his puny action began the independent life of a nation to whose future none dares prescribe limits.

Discovery and colonization were inevitable, and are common to all lands. Civil wars are expressions rather than causes of great crises. Civil and commercial progress are inevitable. But the Declaration of Independence was an act of conscious choice.

No other incident in our history was so momentous, none so dramatic and comprehensive of past and future.

Columbus was an unconscious instrument in opening a new world; the Spanish, French, Dutch, and English explorers were all working toward a consummation none foresaw; the founders of colonies had their ideals, but all have been swallowed up in our national development. The Revolution alone looked both backward and forward, and the fathers of the republic gave us the law of our national being.

The birth-cry of the nation came from the lips of the child who cried aloud in the streets:

Ring! *Ring!* RING!"

THE DECLARATION OF INDEPENDENCE IN THE LIGHT OF MODERN CRITICISM [1]

BY MOSES COIT TYLER

(Professor of History in Cornell University.)

I

It can hardly be doubted that some hindrance to a right estimate of the Declaration of Independence is occasioned by either of two opposite conditions of

[1] *From " The North American Review," 1896.*

mind, both of which are often to be met with among us; on the one hand, a condition of hereditary, uncritical awe and worship of the American Revolution, and of that state paper as its absolutely perfect and glorious expression; on the other hand, a later condition of cultivated distrust of the Declaration, as a piece of writing lifted up into inordinate renown by the passionate and heroic circumstances of its origin, and ever since then extolled beyond reason by the blind energy of patriotic enthusiasm. Turning from the former state of mind, which obviously calls for no further comment, we may note, as a partial illustration of the latter, that American confidence in the supreme intellectual merit of this all-famous document received a serious wound some forty years ago from the hand of Rufus Choate, when, with a courage greater than would now be required for such an act, he characterized it as made up of " glittering and sounding generalities of natural right." What the great advocate then so unhesitatingly suggested, many a thoughtful American since then has at least suspected — that our great proclamation, as a piece of political literature, cannot stand the test of modern analysis; that it belongs to the immense class of over-praised productions; that it is, in fact, a stately patchwork of sweeping propositions of somewhat doubtful validity; that it has long imposed upon mankind by the well-known effectiveness of verbal glitter and sound; that, at the best, it is an example of florid political declamation belonging to the sophomoric period of our national life, a period which, as we flatter ourselves, we have now outgrown.

Nevertheless, it is to be noted that whatever authority the Declaration of Independence has acquired in the world, has been due to no lack of criticism, either at the time of its first appearance, or since then; a fact which seems to tell in favor of its essential worth and strength. From the date of its original publication down to the present moment, it has been attacked again and again, either in anger, or in contempt, by friends as well as by enemies of the American Revolution, by liberals in politics as well as by conservatives. It has been censured for its substance, it has been censured for its form, for its misstatements of fact, for its fallacies in reasoning, for its audacious novelties and paradoxes, for its total lack of all novelty, for its repetition of old and threadbare statements, even for its downright plagiarisms; finally, for its grandiose and vaporing style.

II

One of the earliest and ablest of its assailants was Thomas Hutchinson, the last civil governor of the colony of Massachusetts, who, being stranded in London by the political storm which had blown him thither, published there, in the autumn of 1776, his " Strictures upon the Declaration of the Congress at Philadelphia," wherein, with an unsurpassed knowledge of the origin of the controversy, and with an unsurpassed acumen in the discussion of it, he traverses the entire document, paragraph by paragraph, for the purpose of showing that its allegations in support of American Independence are " false and frivolous."

A better written, and, upon the whole, a more plausible and a more powerful arraignment of the great Declaration was the celebrated pamphlet by Sir John Dalrymple, " The Rights of Great Britain Asserted against the Claims of America: Being an Answer to the Declaration of the General Congress,"— a pamphlet scattered broadcast over the world at such a rate that at least eight editions of it were published during the last three or four months of the year, 1776. Here, again, the manifesto of Congress is subjected to a searching examination, in order to prove that "the facts are either willfully or ignorantly misrepresented, and the arguments deduced from premises that have no foundation in truth." It is doubtful if any disinterested student of history, any competent judge of reasoning, will now deny to this pamphlet the praise of making out a very strong case against the historical accuracy and the logical soundness of many parts of the Declaration of Independence.

Undoubtedly, the force of such censures is for us much broken by the fact that they proceeded from men who were themselves partisans in the Revolutionary controversy, and bitterly hostile to the whole movement which the Declaration was intended to justify. Such is not the case, however, with the leading modern English critics of the same document, who while blaming in severe terms the policy of the British Government toward the Thirteen Colonies, have also found much to abate from the confidence due to this official announcement of the reasons for our secession from the empire. For example, Earl Russell, after frankly saying that the great disruption proclaimed by the Declaration of Independence was a result which Great Britain had "used every means most fitted to bring about," such as "vacillation in council, harshness in language, feebleness in execution, disregard of American sympathies and affections," also pointed out that "the truth of this memorable Declaration" was "warped" by "one singular

defect," namely, its exclusive and excessive arraignment of George the Third, " as a single and despotic
tyrant," much like Philip the Second to the people of
the Netherlands.

This temperate criticism from an able and a liberal
English statesman of the present century may be said
to touch the very core of the problem as to the historic
justice of our great indictment of the last King of
America; and there is deep significance in the fact
that this is the very criticism upon the document,
which, as John Adams tells us, he himself had in mind
when it was first submitted to him in committee, and
even, when, shortly afterward, he advocated its
adoption by Congress. After mentioning certain
things in it with which he was delighted, he adds:

" There were other expressions which I would not
have inserted if I had drawn it up — particularly that
which called the king tyrant. I thought this too personal; for I never believed George to be a tyrant in
disposition and in nature. I always believed him to
be deceived by his courtiers on both sides of the Atlantic, and in his official capacity only cruel. I thought
the expression too passionate, and too much like
scolding, for so grave and solemn a document; but, as
Franklin and Sherman were to inspect it afterwards
I thought it would not become me to strike it out. I
consented to report it."

A more minute and a more poignant criticism of
the Declaration of Independence has been made in
recent years by still another English writer of liberal
tendencies, who, however, in his capacity as critic,
seems here to labor under the disadvantage of having
transferred to the document which he undertakes to
judge much of the extreme dislike which he has for

the man who wrote it, whom, indeed, he regards as a sophist, as a demagogue, as quite capable of inveracity in speech, and as bearing some resemblance to Robespierre "in his feline nature, his malignant egotism, and his intense suspiciousness, as well as in his bloody-minded, yet possibly sincere, philanthropy." In the opinion of Prof. Goldwin Smith, our great national manifesto is written "in a highly rhetorical strain; it opens with sweeping aphorisms about the natural rights of man, at which political science now smiles, and which . . . might seem strange when framed for slave-holding communities by a publicist who himself held slaves"; while, in his specifications of fact, it "is not more scrupulously truthful than are the general utterances" of the statesman who was its scribe. Its charges that the several offensive acts of the king, besides "evincing a design to reduce the colonists under absolute despotism," "all had as their direct object the establishment of an absolute tyranny," are simply "propositions which history cannot accept." Moreover, the Declaration "blinks the fact that many of the acts, styled steps of usurpation, were measures of repression, which, however unwise or excessive, had been provoked by popular outrage. No government could allow its officers to be assaulted and their houses sacked, its loyal lieges to be tarred and feathered, or the property of merchants sailing under its flag to be thrown by lawless hands into the sea." Even "the preposterous violence and the manifest insincerity of the suppressed clause" against slavery and the slave-trade "are enough to create suspicion as to the spirit in which the whole document was framed."

III

Finally, as has been already intimated, not even among Americans themselves has the Declaration of Independence been permitted to pass on into the enjoyment of its superb renown, without much critical disparagement at the hands of statesmen and historians. No doubt Calhoun had its preamble in mind when he declared that "nothing can be more unfounded and false" than "the prevalent opinion that all men are born free and equal"; for "it rests upon the assumption of a fact which is contrary to universal observation." Of course, all Americans who have shared to any extent in Calhoun's doctrines respecting human society could hardly fail to agree with him in regarding as fallacious and worthless those general propositions in the Declaration which seem to constitute its logical starting point, as well as its ultimate defense.

Perhaps, however, the most frequent form of disparagement to which Jefferson's great state paper has been subjected among us is that which would minimize his merit in composing it, by denying to it the merit of originality. For example, Richard Henry Lee sneered at it as a thing "copied from Locke's *Treatise on Government.*" The author of a life of Jefferson, published in the year of Jefferson's retirement from the presidency, suggests that the credit of having composed the Declaration of Independence "has been perhaps more generally, than truly, given by the public" to that great man. Charles Campbell, the historian of Virginia, intimates that some expressions in the document were taken without acknowledgment from Aphra Behn's tragi-comedy,

" The Widow-Ranter, or the History of Bacon in Virginia." John Stockton Littell describes the Declaration of Independence as " that enduring monument at once of patriotism, and of genius and skill in the art of appropriation "— asserting that " for the sentiments and much of the language " of it, Jefferson was indebted to Chief Justice Brayton's charge to the grand jury of Charleston, delivered in April, 1776, as well as to the Declaration of Independence said to have been adopted by some citizens of Mecklenburg County, North Carolina, in May, 1775. Even the latest and most critical editor of the writings of Jefferson calls attention to the fact that a glance at the Declaration of Rights, as adopted by Virginia on the 12th of June, 1776, " would seem to indicate the source from which Jefferson derived a most important and popular part " of his famous production. By no one, however, has the charge of a lack of originality been pressed with so much decisiveness as by John Adams, who took evident pleasure in speaking of it as a document in which were merely " recapitulated " previous and well-known statements of American rights and wrongs, and who, as late as in the year 1822, deliberately wrote:

" There is not an idea in it but what had been hackneyed in Congress for two years before. The substance of it is contained in the declaration of rights and the violation of those rights, in the Journals of Congress, in 1774. Indeed, the essence of it is contained in a pamphlet, voted and printed by the town of Boston, before the first Congress met, composed by James Otis, as I suppose, in one of his lucid intervals, and pruned and polished by Samuel Adams."

IV

Perhaps nowhere in our literature would it be possible to find a criticism brought forward by a really able man against any piece of writing less applicable to the case, and of less force and value, than is this particular criticism by John Adams and others, as to the lack of originality in the Declaration of Independence.   Indeed, for such a paper as Jefferson was commissioned to write, the one quality which it could not properly have had, the one quality which would have been fatal to its acceptance either by the American Congress or by the American people — is originality. They were then at the culmination of a tremendous controversy over alleged grievances of the most serious kind — a controversy that had been steadily raging for at least twelve years.   In the course of that long dispute, every phase of it, whether as to abstract right or constitutional privilege or personal procedure, had been presented in almost every conceivable form of speech.   At last, they had resolved, in view of all this experience, no longer to prosecute the controversy as members of the empire ; they had resolved to revolt, and, casting off forever their ancient fealty to the British crown, to separate from the empire, and to establish themselves as a new nation among the nations of the earth.   In this emergency as it happened, Jefferson was called upon to put into form a suitable statement of the chief considerations which prompted them to this great act of revolution, and which, as they believed, justified it.   What, then, was Jefferson to do?   Was he to regard himself as a mere literary essayist, set to produce before the world a sort of prize-dissertation

— a calm, analytic, judicial treatise on history and politics with a particular application to Anglo-American affairs — one essential merit of which would be its originality as a contribution to historical and political literature? Was he not, rather, to regard himself, as, for the time being, the very mouthpiece and prophet of the people whom he represented, and as such required to bring together and to set in order, in their name, not what was new, but what was old; to gather up into his own soul, as much as possible, whatever was then also in their souls, their very thoughts and passions, their ideas of constitutional law, their interpretations of fact, their opinions as to men and as to events in all that ugly quarrel, their notions of justice, of civic dignity, of human rights; finally, their memories of wrongs which seemed to them intolerable, especially of wrongs inflicted upon them during those twelve years by the hands of insolent and brutal men, in the name of the king, and by his apparent command?

Moreover, as the nature of the task laid upon him made it necessary that he should thus state, as the reasons for their intended act, those very considerations both as to fact and as to opinion which had actually operated upon their minds, so did it require him to do so, to some extent, in the very language which the people themselves, in their more formal and deliberate utterances, had all along been using. In the development of political life in England and America, there had already been created a vast literature of constitutional progress — a literature common to both portions of the English race, pervaded by its own stately traditions, and reverberating certain great phrases which formed, as one may say, almost the vernacular of English justice, and of English aspiration for a free, manly and orderly political life. In this vernacular the Declaration of Independence was written. The phraseology thus characteristic of it is the very phraseology of the champions of constitutional expansion, of civic dignity and progress, within the English race ever since Magna Charta; of the great state papers of English freedom in the seventeenth century, particularly the Petition of Right in 1629, and the Bill of Rights in 1789; of the great English Charters for colonization in America; of the great English exponents of legal and political progress — Sir Edward Coke, John Milton, Sir Philip Sidney, John Locke; finally, of the great American exponents of political liberty, and of the chief representative bodies, whether local or general, which had convened in America from the time of Stamp Act Congress until that of the Congress which resolved upon our independence. To say, therefore, that the official declaration of that resolve is a paper made up of the very opinions, beliefs, unbeliefs, the very sentiments, prejudices, passions, even the errors in judgment and the personal misconstructions — if they were such — which then actually impelled the American people to that mighty act, and that all these are expressed in the very phrases which they had been accustomed to use, is to pay to that state-paper the highest tribute as to its fitness for the purpose for which it was framed.

Of much of this, also, Jefferson himself seems to have been conscious; and perhaps never does he rise before us with more dignity, with more truth, than when, late in his lifetime, hurt by the captious and jangling words of disparagement then recently put into writing by his old comrade, to the effect that the Declaration of Independence " contained no new ideas, that it is a commonplace compilation, its sentences hackneyed in Congress for two years before, and its essence contained in Otis's pamphlet," Jefferson quietly remarked that perhaps these statements might " all be true: of that I am not to be the judge. . . . Whether I had gathered my ideas from reading or reflection, I do not know. I know only that I turned to neither book nor pamphlet while writing it. I did not consider it as any part of my charge to invent new ideas altogether and to offer no sentiment which had ever been expressed before."

Before passing from this phase of the subject, however, it should be added that, while the Declaration of Independence lacks originality in the sense just indicated, in another and perhaps in a higher sense, it possesses originality — it is individualized by the character and by the genius of its author. Jefferson gathered up the thoughts and emotions and even the characteristic phrases of the people for whom he wrote, and these he perfectly incorporated with what was already in his mind, and then to the music of his own keen, rich, passionate, and enkindling style, he mustered them into that stately and triumphant procession wherein, as some of us still think, they will go marching on to the world's end.

There were then in Congress several other men who could have written the Declaration of Independence, and written it well — notably Franklin, either of the two Adamses, Richard Henry Lee, William Livingston, and, best of all, but for his own opposition to the measure, John Dickinson; but had any one of these other men written the Declaration of

Independence, while it would have contained, doubtless, nearly the same topics and nearly the same great formulas of political statement, it would yet have been a wholly different composition from this of Jefferson's. No one at all familiar with his other writings, as well as with the writings of his chief contemporaries, could ever have a moment's doubt, even if the fact were not already notorious, that this document was by Jefferson. He put into it something that was his own, and that no one else could have put there. He put himself into it — his own genius, his own moral force, his faith in God, his faith in ideas, his love of innovation, his passion for progress, his invincible enthusiasm, his intolerance of prescription, of injustice, of cruelty; his sympathy, his clarity of vision, his affluence of diction, his power to fling out great phrases which will long fire and cheer the souls of men struggling against political unrighteousness.

And herein lies its essential originality, perhaps the most precious, and, indeed, almost the only originality ever attaching to any great literary product that is representative of its time. He made for himself no improper claim, therefore, when he directed that upon the granite obelisk at his grave should be carved the words: "Here was buried Thomas Jefferson, author of the Declaration of Independence."

V

If the Declaration of Independence is now to be fairly judged by us, it must be judged with reference to what it was intended to be, namely, an impassioned manifesto of one party, and that the weaker party, in a violent race-quarrel; of a party resolved, at last, upon the extremity of revolution, and already menaced by the inconceivable disaster of being defeated in the very act of armed rebellion against the mightiest military power on earth. This manifesto, then, is not to be censured because, being avowedly a statement of his own side of the quarrel, it does not also contain a moderate and judicial statement of the opposite side; or because, being necessarily partisan in method, it is likewise both partisan and vehement in tone; or because it bristles with accusations against the enemy so fierce and so unqualified as now to seem in some respects overdrawn; or because it resounds with certain great aphorisms about the natural rights of man, at which, indeed, political science cannot now smile, except to its own discomfiture and shame — aphorisms which are likely to abide in this world as the chief source and inspiration of heroic enterprises among men for self-deliverance from oppression.

Taking into account, therefore, as we are bound to do, the circumstances of its origin, and especially its purpose as a solemn and piercing appeal to mankind on behalf of a small and weak nation against the alleged injustice and cruelty of a great and powerful one, it still remains our duty to inquire whether, as has been asserted in our time, history must set aside either of the two central charges embodied in the Declaration of Independence.

The first of these charges affirms that the several acts complained of by the colonists evinced "a design to reduce them under absolute despotism," and had as their "direct object the establishment of an absolute tyranny" over the American people. Was this, indeed, a groundless charge, in the sense in-

tended by the words "despotism" and "tyranny"—
that is, in the sense commonly given to those words
in the usage of the English-speaking race? According to that usage, it was not an Oriental despotism
that was meant, nor a Greek tyranny, nor a Roman,
nor a Spanish. The sort of despot, the sort of tyrant,
whom the English people, ever since the time of King
John and especially during the period of the Stuarts,
had been accustomed to look for and to guard against,
was the sort of tyrant or despot that could be evolved
out of the conditions of English political life. Fur-
thermore, he was not by them expected to appear
among them at the outset in the fully developed shape
of a Philip or an Alva in the Netherlands. They
were able to recognize him, they were prepared to
resist him, in the earliest and most incipient stage
of his being — at the moment, in fact, when he should
make his first attempt to gain all power over his
people, by assuming the single power to take their
property without their consent. Hence it was, as
Edmund Burke pointed out in the House of Commons only a few weeks before the American Revolution entered upon its military phase, that:

"The great contests for freedom . . . were
from the earliest times chiefly upon the question of
taxing. Most of the contests in the ancient com-
monwealths turned primarily on the right of election
of magistrates, or on the balance among the several
orders of the state. The question of money was not
with them so immediate. But in England it was
otherwise. On this point of taxes the ablest pens
and most eloquent tongues have been exercised, the
greatest spirits have acted and suffered. . . .
They took infinite pains to inculcate, as a funda-

mental principle, that in all monarchies the people must in effect, themselves, mediately or immediately, possess the power of granting their own money, or no shadow of liberty could subsist. The colonies draw from you, as with their life-blood, these ideas and principles. Their love of liberty, as with you, fixed and attached on this specific point of taxing. Liberty might be safe or might be endangered in twenty other particulars without their being much pleased or alarmed. Here they felt its pulse, and as they found that beat, they thought themselves sick or sound."

Accordingly, the meaning which the English race on both sides of the Atlantic were accustomed to attach to the words " tyranny " and " despotism," was a meaning to some degree ideal; it was a meaning drawn from the extraordinary political sagacity with which the race is endowed, from their extraordinary sensitiveness as to the use of the taxing-power in government, from their instinctive perception of the commanding place of the taxing-power among all the other forms of power in the state, from their perfect assurance that he who holds the purse with the power to fill it and to empty it, holds the key of the situation — can maintain an army of his own, can rule without consulting Parliament, can silence criticism, can crush opposition, can strip his subjects of every vestige of political life; in other words, he can make slaves of them, he can make a despot and a tyrant of himself. Therefore, the system which in the end might develop into results so palpably tyrannic and despotic, they bluntly called a tyranny and a despotism in the beginning. To say, therefore, that the Declaration of Independence did the same, is to say that it spoke good English. Of course, history will be ready to set aside the charge thus made in language not at all liable to be misunderstood, just so soon as history is ready to set aside the common opinion that the several acts of the British government, from 1764 to 1776, for laying and enforcing taxation in America, did evince a somewhat particular and systematic design to take away some portion of the property of the American people without their consent.

The second of the two great charges contained in the Declaration of Independence, while intimating that some share in the blame is due to the British Parliament and to the British people, yet fastens upon the king himself as the one person chiefly responsible for the scheme of American tyranny therein set forth, and culminates in the frank description of him as " a prince whose character is thus marked by every act which may define a tyrant." Is this accusation of George the Third now to be set aside as unhistoric? Was that king, or was he not, chiefly responsible for the American policy of the British government between the years 1764 and 1776? If he was so, then the historic soundness of the most important portion of the Declaration of Independence is vindicated.

Fortunately, this question can be answered without hesitation, and in a few words; and for these few words, an American writer of to-day, conscious of his own bias of nationality, will rightly prefer to cite such words as have been uttered upon the subject by the ablest English historians of our time. Upon their statements alone it must be concluded that George the Third ascended his throne with the fixed purpose of resuming to the crown many of those powers which, by the constitution of England, did not then belong to it, and that in this purpose, at least during the first twenty-five years of his reign, he substantially succeeded — himself determining what should be the policy of each administration, what opinions his ministers should advocate in Parliament, and what measures Parliament itself should adopt. Says Sir Erskine May:

" The king desired to undertake personally the chief administration of public affairs, to direct the policy of his ministers, and himself to distribute the patronage of the crown. He was ambitious not only to reign, but to govern. Strong as were the ministers, the king was resolved to wrest all power from their hands, and to exercise it himself. But what was this in effect but to assert that the king should be his own minister? . . . The king's tactics were fraught with danger, as well to the crown itself as to the constitutional liberties of the people."

Already prior to the year 1778, according to Lecky, the king had "laboriously built up " in England a " system of personal government "; and it was because he was unwilling to have this system disturbed that he then refused, " in defiance of the most earnest representations of his own minister and of the most eminent politicians of every party . . . to send for the greatest of living statesmen at the moment when the empire appeared to be in the very agonies of dissolution. . . . Either Chatham or Rockingham should have insisted that the policy of the country should be directed by its responsible ministers and not dictated by an irresponsible sovereign."

This refusal of the king to pursue the course which was called for by the constitution, and which would have taken the control of the policy of the government out of his hands, was, according to the same great historian, an act " the most criminal in the whole reign of George the Third; . . . as criminal as any of those acts which led Charles the First to the scaffold."

Even so early as the year 1768, according to John Richard Green,

"George the Third had at last reached his aim. . . . In the early days of the ministry " (which began in that year) " his influence was felt to be predominant. In its later and more disastrous days it was supreme; for Lord North, who became the head of the ministry on Grafton's retirement in 1770, was the mere mouthpiece of the king. ' Not only did he direct the minister,' a careful observer tells us, ' in all important matters of foreign and domestic policy, but he instructed him as to the management of debates in Parliament, suggested what motions should be made or opposed, and how measures should be carried. He reserved for himself all the patronage, he arranged the whole cast of the administration, settled the relative place and pretentions of ministers of state, law officers, and members of the household, nominated and promoted the English and Scotch judges, appointed and translated bishops and deans, and dispensed other preferments in the church. He disposed of military governments, regiments, and commissions, and himself ordered the marching of troops. He gave and refused titles, honors, and pensions.' All this immense patronage was steadily used for the creation of a party in both houses of Parliament attached to the king himself. . . . George, was, in fact, sole minister during the fifteen years which followed; and the shame of the darkest hour of English history lies wholly at his door."

Surely, until these tremendous verdicts of English history shall be set aside, there need be no anxiety in any quarter as to the historic soundness of the two great accusations which together make up the principal portion of the Declaration of Independence. In the presence of these verdicts also, even the passion, the intensity of language, in which those accusations are uttered, seem to find a perfect justification. Indeed, in the light of the most recent and most unprejudiced expert testimony, the whole document, both in its substance and in its form, seems to have been the logical response of a nation of brave men to the great words of the greatest of English statesmen, as spoken in the House of Commons precisely ten years before:

" This kingdom has no right to lay a tax on the colonies. Sir, I rejoice that America has resisted. Three millions of people, so dead to all the feelings of liberty as voluntarily to submit to be slaves, would have been fit instruments to make slaves of the rest."

VI

Thus, ever since its first announcement to the world, and down almost to the present moment, has the Declaration of Independence been tested by criticism of every possible kind — by criticism intended and expected to be destructive. Apparently, however, all this criticism has failed to accomplish its object.

It is proper for us to remember, also, that what we call criticism is not the only valid test of the genuineness and worth of any piece of writing of great practical interest to mankind; there is, in addition, the test of actual use and service, in direct contact with the common sense and the moral sense of large masses of men, under various conditions, and for a long period. Probably no writing which is not essentially sound and true has ever survived this test.

Neither from this test has the great Declaration any need to shrink. As to the immediate use for which it was sent forth — that of rallying and uniting the friends of the Revolution, and bracing them for their great task — its effectiveness was so great and so obvious that it has never been denied. During the century and a quarter since the Revolution, its influence on the political character and the political conduct of the American people has been great beyond calculation. For example, after we had achieved our own national deliverance, and had advanced into that enormous and somewhat corrupting material prosperity which followed the adoption of the constitution and the development of the cotton-interest and the expansion of the Republic into a transcontinental power, we fell under an appalling temptation — the temptation to forget, or to repudiate, or to refuse to apply to the case of our human brethren in bondage, the principles which we had once proclaimed as the basis of every rightful government. The prodigious service rendered to us in this awful moral emergency by the Declaration of Independence, was, that its public repetition, at least once every year, in the hearing of vast throngs of the American people in every portion of the Republic, kept constantly before our minds, in a form of almost religious sanctity, those few great ideas as to the dignity of human nature, and the sacredness of personality, and the indestructible rights of man as mere man, with which it had so gloriously identified the beginnings of our national existence. It did at last become very hard for us to listen each year to the preamble of the Declaration and still remain the owners and users and catchers of slaves; still harder, to accept the doctrine that the righteousness and prosperity of slavery was to be accepted as the dominant policy of the nation. The logic of Calhoun was as flawless as usual, when he concluded that the chief obstruction in the way of his system was the preamble of the Declaration of Independence. Had it not been for the inviolable sacredness given by it to those sweeping aphorisms about the natural rights of man, it may be doubted whether Calhoun might not have won over an immense majority of the American people to the support of his compact and plausible scheme for making slavery the basis of the Republic. It was the preamble of the Declaration of Independence which elected Lincoln, which sent forth the Emancipation Proclamation, which gave victory to Grant, which ratified the Thirteenth Amendment.

We shall not here attempt to delineate the influence of this state paper upon mankind in general. Of course, the emergence of the American Republic as an imposing world-power is a phenomenon which has now for many years attracted the attention of the human race. Surely, no slight effect must have resulted from the fact that, among all civilized peoples, the one American document best known is the Declaration of Independence, and that thus the spectacle of so vast and beneficent a political success has been everywhere associated with the assertion of the natural rights of man. " The doctrines it contained," says Buckle, " were not merely welcomed by a majority of the French nation, but even the government itself was unable to withstand the general feeling. Its effect in hastening the approach of the French Revolution . . . was indeed most remarkable." Elsewhere, also, in many lands, among many peoples, it has been cited again and again as an inspiration to political courage, as a model for political conduct; and if, as the brilliant historian just alluded to has affirmed, " that noble Declaration . . . ought to be hung up in the nursery of every king, and blazoned on the porch of every royal palace," it is because it has become the classic statement of political truths which must at last abolish kings altogether, or else teach them to identify their existence with the dignity and happiness of human nature.

V

THE STRUGGLE FOR INDEPENDENCE

THE PRINCIPLES OF THE REVOLUTION

BY JOSIAH QUINCY

WHEN we speak of the glory of our fathers, we mean not that vulgar renown to be attained by physical strength; nor yet that higher fame, to be acquired by intellectual power. Both often exist without lofty thought, pure intent, or generous purpose. The glory which we celebrate was strictly of a moral and religious character: righteous as to its ends; just as to its means.

The American Revolution had its origin neither in ambition, nor avarice, nor envy, nor in any gross passion; but in the nature and relation of things, and in the thence-resulting necessity of separation from the parent state. Its progress was limited by that necessity. Our fathers displayed great strength and great moderation of purpose. In difficult times they conducted it with wisdom; in doubtful times, with firmness; in perilous times, with courage; under oppressive trials, erect; amidst temptations, unseduced; in the dark hour of danger, fearless; in the bright hour of prosperity, faithful.

It was not the instant feeling and pressure of despotism that roused them to resist, but the principle on which that arm was extended. They could have paid the impositions of the British government, had they been increased a thousandfold; but payment acknowledged right, and they spurned the consequences of that acknowledgment. But, above all, they realized that those burdens, though light in themselves, would to coming ages — to us, their posterity — be heavy, and probably insupportable. They preferred to meet the trial in their own times, and to make the sacrifices in their own persons, that we and our descendants, their posterity, might reap the harvest and enjoy the increase.

Generous men, exalted patriots, immortal statesmen! For this deep moral and social affection, for this elevated self-devotion, this bold daring, the multiplying millions of your posterity, as they spread backward to the lakes, and from the lakes to the mountains, and from the mountains to the western waters, shall annually, in all future time, come up to the temples of the Most High, with song and anthem, and thanksgiving; with cheerful symphonies and hallelujahs, to repeat your names; to look steadfastly on the brightness of your glory; to trace its spreading rays to the points from which they emanate; and to seek in your character and conduct a practical illustration of public duty in every occurring social exigency.

THE SONG OF THE CANNON

BY SAM WALTER FOSS

WHEN the diplomats cease from their capers,
　　Their red-tape requests and replies,
Their shuttlecock battle of papers,
　　Their saccharine parley of lies;
When the plenipotentiary wrangle
　　Is tied in a chaos of knots,

And becomes an unwindable tangle
  Of verbals unmarried to thoughts;
When they've anguished and argued profoundly,
  Asserted, assumed, and averred,
Then I end up the dialogue roundly
  With my monosyllabical word.

Not mine in a speech academic,
  No lexicon lingo is mine,
And in politic parley, polemic,
  I was never created to shine.
But I speak with some show of decision,
  And I never attempt to be bland,
I hurl my one word with precision,
  My hearers — they all understand.
It requires no labored translation,
  Its pith and its import to glean;
They gather its signification;
  They know at the first what I mean.

The codes of the learned legations,
  Of form, and of rule, and decree,
The etiquette books of the nations,—
  They were never intended for me.
When your case is talked into confusion,
  Then hush you, my diplomat friend,
Give me just a word in conclusion,
  Let me bring the dispute to an end.
Ye diplomats, cease to aspire,
  A case that's appealed to debate,
It has gone to a court that is higher,
  And I'm the Attorney for Fate.

PAUL REVERE'S RIDE [1]

(April 18, 1775.)

BY HENRY WADSWORTH LONGFELLOW

LISTEN, my children, and you shall hear
Of the midnight ride of Paul Revere,
On the eighteenth of April, in Seventy-Five:
Hardly a man is now alive
Who remembers that famous day and year.

He said to his friend, " If the British march
By land or sea from the town to-night,
Hang a lantern aloft in the belfry arch
Of the North Church tower as a signal-light,
One, if by land, and two, if by sea;
And I on the opposite shore will be,
Ready to ride and spread the alarm
Through every Middlesex village and farm,
For the country folk to be up and to arm."

Then he said, good night! and with muffled oar
Silently rowed to the Charlestown shore,
Just as the moon rose over the bay,
Where swinging wide at her moorings lay
The Somerset, British man-of-war;
A phantom ship, with each mast and spar
Across the moon like a prison-bar,
And a huge black hulk, that was magnified
By its own reflection in the tide.

[1] *By permission of the publishers, Houghton, Mifflin Co.*

Meanwhile, his friend, through alley and street
Wanders and watches with eager ears,
Till in the silence around him he hears
The muster of men at the barrack door,
The sound of arms, and the tramp of feet,
And the measured tread of the grenadiers,
Marching down to their boats on the shore.

Then he climbed to the tower of the Old North
    Church,
By the wooden stairs, with stealthy tread,
To the belfry-chamber overhead,
And startled the pigeons from their perch
On the somber rafters, that round him made
Masses and moving shapes of shade,—
By the trembling ladder, steep and tall,
To the highest window in the wall,
Where he paused to listen and look down
A moment on the roofs of the town,
And the moonlight flowing over all.

Beneath, in the churchyard, lay the dead,
In their night-encampment on the hill,
Wrapped in silence so deep and still,
That he could hear, like a sentinel's tread,
The watchful night-wind, as it went
Creeping along from tent to tent,
And seeming to whisper, " All is well ! "
A moment only he feels the spell
Of the place and the hour, and the secret dread
Of the lonely belfry and the dead ;
For suddenly all his thoughts are bent

On a shadowy something far away,
Where the river widens to meet the bay,
A line of black that bends and floats
On the rising tide, like a bridge of boats.

Meanwhile, impatient to mount and ride,
Booted and spurred, with a heavy stride
On the opposite shore walked Paul Revere.
Now he patted his horse's side,
Now gazed at the landscape far and near,
Then, impetuous, stamped the earth,
And turned and tightened his saddle-girth;
But mostly he watched with eager search
The belfry-tower of the Old North Church,
As it rose above the graves on the hill,
Lonely, and spectral, and somber and still.
And lo! as he looks, on the belfry's height
A glimmer, and then a gleam of light!
He springs to the saddle, the bridle he turns,
But lingers and gazes, till full on his sight
A second lamp in the belfry burns!
A hurry of hoofs in a village street,
A shape in the moonlight, a bulk in the dark,
And beneath, from the pebbles, in passing, a spark
Struck out by a steed flying fearless and fleet:
That was all! And yet, through the gloom and the
        light,
The fate of a nation was riding that night;
And the spark struck out by that steed, in his flight,
Kindled the land into flame with its heat.

He has left the village and mounted the steep,
And beneath him, tranquil and broad and deep

Is the Mystic, meeting the ocean tides;
And under the alders, that skirt its edge,
Now soft on the sand, now loud on the ledge,
Is heard the tramp of his steed as he rides.

It was twelve by the village clock
When he crossed the bridge into Medford town.
He heard the crowing of the cock,
And the barking of the farmer's dog,
And felt the damp of the river fog,
That rises after the sun goes down.

It was one by the village clock,
When he rode into Lexington.
He saw the gilded weathercock
Swim in the moonlight as he passed,
And the meeting-house windows, blank and bare,
Gaze at him with a spectral glare,
As if they already stood aghast
At the bloody work they would look upon.

It was two by the village clock,
When he came to the bridge in Concord town,
He heard the bleating of the flock,
And the twitter of birds among the trees,
And felt the breath of the morning breeze
Blowing over the meadows brown.
And one was safe and asleep in his bed
Who at the bridge would be first to fall,
Who that day would be lying dead,
Pierced by a British musket-ball.

You know the rest. In the books you have read,
How the British Regulars fired and fled,—
How the farmers gave them ball for ball,
From behind each fence and farm-yard wall,
Chasing the red-coats down the lane,
Then crossing the fields to emerge again
Under the trees at the turn of the road,
And only pausing to fire and load.

So through the night rode Paul Revere;
And so through the night went his cry of alarm
To every Middlesex village and farm,—
A cry of defiance and not of fear,
A voice in the darkness, a knock at the door,
And a word that shall echo forevermore!
For, borne on the night-wind of the Past,
Through all our history, to the last,
In the hour of darkness and peril and need,
The people will waken and listen to hear
The hurrying hoof-beats of that steed,
And the midnight message of Paul Revere.

HYMN

BY RALPH WALDO EMERSON

(This poem was written to be sung at the completion of the Concord Monument, April 19, 1836.)

By the rude bridge that arched the flood,
    Their flag to April's breeze unfurled,
Here once the embattled farmers stood,
    And fired the shot heard round the world.

The foe long since in silence slept;
   Alike the conqueror silent sleeps;
And Time the ruined bridge has swept
   Down the dark stream which seaward creeps.

On this green bank, by this soft stream,
   We set to-day a votive stone;
That memory may their deed redeem
   When, like our sires, our sons are gone.

Spirit, that made those heroes dare
   To die, or leave their children free,
Bid Time and Nature gently spare
   The shaft we raise to them and thee.

A SONG FOR LEXINGTON

BY ROBERT KELLEY WEEKS

THE spring came earlier on
Than usual that year;
The shadiest snow was gone,
The slowest brook was clear,
And warming in the sun
Shy flowers began to peer.

'Twas more like middle May,
The earth so seemed to thrive,
That Nineteenth April day
Of Seventeen Seventy-Five;
Winter was well away,
New England was alive!

Alive and sternly glad!
Her doubts were with the snow;
Her courage, long forbade,
Ran full to overflow;
And every hope she had
Began to bud and grow.

She rose betimes that morn,
For there was work to do;
A planting, not of corn,
Of what she hardly knew,—
Blessings for men unborn;
And well she did it, too!

With open hand she stood,
And sowed for all the years,
And watered it with blood,
And watered it with tears,
The seed of quickening food
For both the hemispheres.

This was the planting done
That April morn of fame;
Honor to every one
To that seed-field that came!
Honor to Lexington,
Our first immortal name!

THE REVOLUTIONARY ALARM

BY GEORGE BANCROFT

DARKNESS closed upon the country and upon the town, but it was no night for sleep. Heralds on swift relays of horses transmitted the war-message from hand to hand, till village repeated it to village; the sea to the backwoods; the plains to the highlands; and it was never suffered to droop till it had been borne North and South, and East and West, throughout the land.

It spread over the bays that receive the Saco and the Penobscot. Its loud reveille broke the rest of the trappers of New Hampshire, and, ringing like bugle-notes from peak to peak, overleapt the Green Mountains, swept onward to Montreal, and descended the ocean river, till the responses were echoed from the cliffs of Quebec. The hills along the Hudson told to one another the tale.

As the summons hurried to the south, it was one day at New York; in one more at Philadelphia; the next it lighted a watchfire at Baltimore; thence it waked an answer at Annapolis. Crossing the Potomac near Mount Vernon, it was sent forward without a halt to Williamsburg. It traversed the Dismal Swamp to Nansemond, along the route of the first emigrants to North Carolina. It moved onwards and still onwards, through boundless groves of evergreen, to New-Berne and to Wilmington.

"For God's sake, forward it by night and by day," wrote Cornelius Harnett, by the express which sped for Brunswick. Patriots of South Carolina caught up its tones at the border and despatched it to Charleston, and through pines and palmettos and moss-clad live-oaks, farther to the south, till it resounded among the New England settlements beyond Savannah.

The Blue Ridge took up the voice, and made it heard from one end to the other of the valley of Virginia. The Alleghanies, as they listened, opened their barriers, that the "loud call" might pass through to the hardy riflemen on the Holston, the Watauga, and the French Broad. Ever renewing its strength, powerful enough even to create a commonwealth, it breathed its inspiring word to the first settlers of Kentucky; so that hunters who made their halt in the matchless valley of the Elkhorn commemorated the 19th day of April, 1775, by naming their encampment *Lexington.*

With one impulse the colonies sprung to arms; with one spirit they pledged themselves to each other " to be ready for the extreme event." With one heart the continent cried, " Liberty or Death! "

THE VOLUNTEER

BY ELBRIDGE JEFFERSON CUTLER

" At dawn," he said, " I bid them all farewell,
  To go where bugles call and rifles gleam."
And with the restless thought asleep he fell,
  And glided into dream.

A great hot plain from sea to mountain spread,—
  Through it a level river slowly drawn;
He moved with a vast crowd, and at its head
  Streamed banners like the dawn.

There came a blinding flash, a deafening roar,
  And dissonant cries of triumph and dismay;
Blood trickled down the river's reedy shore,
  And with the dead he lay.

The morn broke in upon his solemn dreams,
  And still with steady pulse and deepening eye,
" Where bugles call," he said, " and rifles gleam,
  I follow, though I die ! "

Wise youth ! By few is glory's wreath attained ;
  But death, or late or soon, awaiteth all,
To fight in Freedom's cause is something gained,—
  And nothing lost to fall.

TICONDEROGA

(May 10, 1775.)

BY V. B. WILSON

The cold, gray light of the dawning
  On old Carillon falls,
And dim in the mist of the morning
  Stand the grim old fortress walls.
No sound disturbs the stillness
  Save the cataract's mellow roar,
Silent as death is the fortress,
  Silent the misty shore.

But up from the wakening waters
  Comes the cool, fresh morning breeze
Lifting the banner of Britain,
  And whispering to the trees
Of the swift gliding boats on the waters
  That are nearing the fog-shrouded land,
With the old Green Mountain Lion,
  And his daring patriot band.

But the sentinel at the postern
    Heard not the whisper low;
He is dreaming of the banks of the Shannon
    As he walks on his beat to and fro,
Of the starry eyes in Green Erin
    That were dim when he marched away,
And a tear down his bronzed cheek courses,
    'Tis the first for many a day.

A sound breaks the misty stillness,
    And quickly he glances around;
Through the mist, forms like towering giants
    Seem rising out of the ground;
A challenge, the firelock flashes,
    A sword cleaves the quivering air,
And the sentry lies dead by the postern,
    Blood staining his bright yellow hair.

Then, with a shout that awakens
    All the echoes of hillside and glen,
Through the low, frowning gate of the fortress,
    Sword in hand, rush the Green Mountain men.
The scarce wakened troops of the garrison
    Yield up their trust pale with fear;
And down comes the bright British banner,
    And out rings a Green Mountain cheer.

Flushed with pride, the whole eastern heavens
    With crimson and gold are ablaze;
And up springs the sun in his splendor
    And flings down his arrowy rays,

Bathing in sunlight the fortress,
　Turning to gold the grim walls,
While louder and clearer and higher
　Rings the song of the waterfalls.

Since the taking of Ticonderoga
　A century has rolled away;
But with pride the nation remembers
　That glorious morning in May.
And the cataract's silvery music
　Forever the story tells,
Of the capture of old Carillon,
　The chime of the silver bells.

WARREN'S ADDRESS

(At the Battle of Bunker Hill.)

BY JOHN PIERPONT

STAND! the ground's your own, my braves!
Will ye give it up to slaves?
Will ye look for greener graves?
　Hope ye mercy still?
What's the mercy despots feel?
Hear it in that battle peal!
Read it on yon bristling steel!
　Ask it,—ye who will!

Fear ye foes who kill for hire?
Will ye to your homes retire?
Look behind you! they're afire,
　And, before you, see

Who have done it! — From the vale
On they come! — and will ye quail? —
Leaden rain and leaden hail
   Let their welcome be!

In the God of battles trust!
Die we may,— and die we must;
But oh, where can dust to dust
   Be consigned so well,
As where Heaven its dews shall shed
On the martyred patriot's bed,
And the rocks shall raise their head
   Of his deeds to tell!

"THE LONELY BUGLE GRIEVES"

(From an "Ode on the Celebration of the Battle of Bunker
Hill, June 17, 1825.")

BY GRENVILLE MELLEN

THE trump hath blown,
   And now upon that reeking hill
Slaughter rides screaming on the vengeful ball;
   While with terrific signal shrill,
The vultures, from their bloody eyries flown,
   Hang o'er them like a pall.
Now deeper roll the maddening drums,
   And the mingling host like ocean heaves:
   While from the midst a horrid wailing comes,
And high above the fight the lonely bugle grieves!

THE BATTLE OF BUNKER HILL

(From "Battles of the American Revolution.")

THE advance of the British army was like a solemn pageant in its steady headway, and like a parade for inspection in the completeness of its outfit. It moved forward as if by the very force of its closely-knit columns it must sweep away every barrier in its path. Elated, sure of victory, with firm step, already quickened as the space of separation lessens, there is left but a few rods of interval, a few steps only, and the work is done! But right in their way was a calm, intense, and energizing love of liberty, represented by men of the same blood and of equal daring.

A few shots impulsively fired, but quickly restrained, drew an innocent fire from the advancing column. But the pale men behind the scant defense, obedient to one will, answered not. . . . The left wing is near the redoubt. It surely is nothing to surmount a bank of fresh earth but six feet high; and its sands and clods can almost be counted, it is so near, so easy, *sure!* Short, crisp, and earnest, low-toned, but felt as an electric pulse from redoubt to river, are the words of a single man, Prescott. Warren, by his side, repeats them. The word runs quickly along the impatient line. The eager fingers give back from the waiting trigger. "Steady, men! Wait until you see the white of the eye! Not a shot sooner! Aim at the handsome coats! Aim at the waistbands! Pick off the officers! Wait for the word, every man! Steady!"

Already those plain men, so patient, can count the

buttons, can read the emblems on the belt-plate, can recognize the officers and men whom they have seen at parade on Boston Common. Features grow more and more distinct. The silence is awful! These men seem breathless,— dead! It comes, that word, the word waited for,—" Fire!" That word had waited behind the center and the left wing, where Putnam watched, as it lingered behind breastwork and redoubt. Sharp, clear, and deadly, in tone and essence, it rings forth,— " Fire!"

From redoubt to river, along the whole sweep of devouring flame, the forms of men wither as in a furnace heat. The whole front goes down. For an instant the chirp of the grasshopper and the cricket in the freshly-cut grass might almost be heard; then the groans of the suffering; then the shouts of impatient yeomen, who leap over obstacles to pursue until recalled to silence and to duty.

Staggering but reviving, grand in the glory of their manhood, heroic in the fortitude which restores self-possession, with a steady step, in the face of fire and over the bodies of their dead, the remnant dare to renew battle. Again the deadly volley; and the shattered columns, in spite of entreaty or command, move back to the place of starting, and the first shock of battle is over.

A lifetime when it is past seems but as a moment! A moment sometimes is as a lifetime. Onset and repulse! Three hundred lifetimes ended in twenty minutes!

THE MARYLAND BATTALION

BY JOHN WILLIAMSON PALMER

Spruce Macaronis, and pretty to see,
Tidy and dapper and gallant were we;
Blooded, fine gentlemen, proper and tall,
Bold in a fox-hunt and gay at a ball;
Prancing soldados so martial and bluff,
Billets for bullets, in scarlet and buff —
But our cockades were clasped with a mother's low
   prayer,
And the sweethearts that braided the sword-knots were
   fair.

There was grummer of drums humming hoarse in the
   hills,
And the bugle sang fanfaron down by the mills;
By Flatbush the bagpipes were droning amain,
And keen cracked the rifles in Martense's lane;
For the Hessians were flecking the hedges with red,
And the grenadiers' tramp marked the roll of the dead.

Three to one, flanked and rear, flashed the files of St.
   George.
The fierce gleam of their steel as the glow of a forge.
The brutal boom-boom of their swart cannoneers
Was sweet music compared with the taunt of their
   cheers —
For the brunt of their onset, our crippled array,
And the light of God's leading gone out in the fray!

Oh, the rout on the left and the tug on the right!
The mad plunge of the charge and the wreck of the
   flight!
When the cohorts of Grant held stout Stirling at strain,
And the mongrels of Hesse went tearing the slain;
When at Freeke's Mill the flumes and the sluices ran
   red,
And the dead choked the dyke and the marsh choked
   the dead!

" O Stirling, good Stirling! how long must we wait?
Shall the shout of your trumpet unleash us too late?
Have you never a dash for brave Mordecai Gist,
With his heart in his throat, and his blade in his fist?
Are we good for no more than to prance in a ball,
When the drums beat the charge and the clarions
   call? "

Tralara! Tralara! Now praise we the Lord
For the clang of His call and the flash of His sword!
Tralara! Tralara! Now forward to die;
For the banner, hurrah! and for sweethearts, good-
   by!
" Four hundred wild lads! " Maybe so. I'll be bound
'Twill be easy to count us, face up, on the ground.
If we hold the road open, tho' Death take the toll,
We'll be missed on parade when the States call the
   roll —
When the flags meet in peace and the guns are at rest,
And fair Freedom is singing Sweet Home in the West.

THE BATTLE OF TRENTON

(Dec. 26, 1776.)

ANONYMOUS AND CONTEMPORARY

On Christmas-day in seventy-six,
Our ragged troops with bayonets fixed,
   For Trenton march away.
The Delaware see! the boats below!
The light obscured by hail and snow!
   But no signs of dismay.

Our object was the Hessian band,
That dared invade fair freedom's land,
   And quarter in that place.
Great Washington he led us on,
Whose streaming flag, in storm or sun,
   Had never known disgrace.

In silent march we passed the night,
Each soldier panting for the fight,
   Though quite benumbed with frost.
Greene, on the left, at six began,
The right was led by Sullivan,
   Who ne'er a moment lost.

The pickets stormed, the alarm was spread,
The rebels risen from the dead
   Were marching into town.
Some scampered here, some scampered there,
And some for action did prepare;
   But soon their arms laid down.

Twelve hundred servile miscreants,
With all their colors, guns, and tents,
  Were trophies of the day.
The frolic o'er, the bright canteen
In center, front, and rear was seen
  Driving fatigue away.

Now brothers of the patriot bands,
Let's sing deliverance from the hands
  Of arbitrary sway,
And as our life is but a span,
Let's touch the tankard while we can,
  In memory of that day.

COLUMBIA

BY TIMOTHY DWIGHT

(Written during the author's services as an army chaplain, 1777–78.)

COLUMBIA, Columbia, to glory arise,
The queen of the world, and the child of the skies;
Thy genius commands thee; with rapture behold,
While ages on ages thy splendor unfold!
Thy reign is the last, and the noblest of time,
Most fruitful thy soil, most inviting thy clime;
Let the crimes of the East ne'er encrimson thy name,
Be freedom, and science, and virtue thy fame.

To conquest and slaughter let Europe aspire;
Whelm nations in blood, and wrap cities in fire;
Thy heroes the rights of mankind shall defend,
And triumph pursue them, and glory attend;

A world is thy realm: for a world be thy laws,
Enlarged as thine empire, and just as thy cause;
On Freedom's broad basis, that empire shall rise,
Extend with the main, and dissolve with the skies.

Fair science her gates to thy sons shall unbar,
And the east shall with morn hide the beams of her
    star.
New bards, and new sages, unrivaled shall soar
To fame unextinguished, when time is no more;
To thee, the last refuge of virtue designed,
Shall fly, from all nations the best of mankind;
Here, grateful to heaven, with transport shall bring
Their incense, more fragrant than odors of spring.

Nor less shall thy fair ones to glory ascend,
And genius and beauty in harmony blend;
The graces of form shall awake pure desire,
And the charms of the soul ever cherish the fire;
Their sweetness unmingled, their manners refined,
The virtue's bright image, instamped on the mind,
With peace and soft rapture shall teach life to glow,
And light up a smile in the aspect of woe.

Thy fleets to all regions thy power shall display,
The nations admire and the ocean obey;
Each shore to thy glory its tribute unfold,
And the East and the South yield their spices and gold.
As the day-spring unbounded, thy splendor shall flow,
And earth's little kingdoms before thee shall bow;
While the ensigns of union, in triumph unfurled,
Hush the tumult of war and give peace to the world.

Thus, as down a lone valley, with cedars o'erspread,
From war's dread confusion I pensively strayed,
The gloom from the face of fair heaven retired;
The winds ceased to murmur; the thunders expired;
Perfumes as of Eden flowed sweetly along,
And a voice as of angels enchantingly sung:
" Columbia, Columbia, to glory arise,
The queen of the world, and the child of the skies."

THE FIGHTING PARSON [1]

BY HENRY AMES BLOOD

IT was brave young Parson Webster,
  His father a parson before him,
And here in this town of Temple
  The people used to adore him;
And the minute-men from all quarters
  That morning had grounded their arms
'Round the meeting-house on the hilltop,
  Looking down on Temple farms.

Dear to the Puritan soldier
  The food which his meeting-house offered,
And especially dear the fine manna
  Which the young Temple minister proffered;
And believe as he might in his firelock,
  His bayonet, or his sword,
The minute-man's heart was hopeless
  If not filled with the strength of the Lord.

[1] *The Century Co., N. Y., publishers.*

The minute-man ever and always
  Waited the signal of warning,
And he never dreamed in the evening
  Where his prayers would ascend the next morn-
    ing;
And they even said that the parson
  Undoubtedly preached his best
When his musket stood in the pulpit
  Ready for use with the rest.

Sad was the minister's message,
  And many a heart beat faster,
And many a soft eye glistened,
  Whenever the voice of the pastor
Dwelt on the absent dear ones
  Who had followed their country's call
To the distant camp, or the battle,
  Or the frowning fortress-wall.

And now when near to " fifteenthly,"
  And the urchins thought of their luncheon,
And into the half-curtained windows
  Hotter and hotter the sun shone,
And the redbreast dozed in the branches,
  And the crow on the pine tree's top,
And the squirrel was lost in his musings,
  The sermon came to a stop.

For sharp on the turnpike the clatter
  Of galloping hoofs resounded,
And the granite ring of the roadway
  Louder and louder sounded;

And now no longer the redbreast
　　Was inclined to be dull that day,
And now no longer the sexton
　　Slept in his usual way.

But all sprang up on the instant,
　　And the widest of eyes grew wider,
While on towards the porch, like a tempest,
　　Came sweeping the horse and its rider;
And now from the din of the hoof-beats
　　A trumpet voice leapt out,
And, tingling to its rafters,
　　The church was alive with the shout,—

" Burgoyne's at Ticonderoga:
　　Would you have the old fort surrender? "
" No, no ! " cried the parson; " New Hampshire
　　Will send the last man to defend her ! "
But before he could shoulder his musket
　　A Tory sang up from below,
" I hear a great voice out of heaven, sir,
　　Warning us not to go."

Quick from the pulpit descending,
　　With the agile step of a lion,—
"᾿The voice you hear is from hell, sir ! "
　　Replied the young servant of Zion.
And out through the open doorway,
　　And on past the porch he strode,
And the congregation came after,
　　And gathered beside the road.

Sadly enough the colonel,
    The minute-men all arraying,
From the dusty cocked hat of the rider
    Drew the lots for going or staying.
Then waving his hat as he took it,
    And putting the spurs to his mare,
The stranger rode off to New Ipswich
    In a cheering that rent the air.

Worse than the shock of battle,
    Now came the sad leave-taking,
'And to mothers and maids and matrons
    The deepest of grief and heart-aching;
And far on the road through the mountains
    Whence the rider had just come,
They followed the minute-men marching
    To the sound of the fife and the drum.

Long dead have they been who sat there
    At that feast of things eternal —
Long dead the laymen, the deacons,
    The lawyer, the doctor, the colonel;
Long dead the youths and the maidens,
    And long on the graves of all
Have the summers and the winters
    Their leaves and their snows let fall.

But whenever I come to the churchyard,
    Where, by the side of the pastor,
They afterwards laid the colonel,
    His friend in success and disaster,

I see again on the Common
The minute-men all in array,
And again I behold the departure,
The pastor leading the way.

And I think of the scene when his comrades
Brought back the young pastor, dying,
To his home in the house of the colonel;
And how, on his death-bed lying,
He took the hand that was offered,
And, gazing far into the night,
Whispered, " I die for my country —
I have fought — I have fought the good fight."

THE SARATOGA LESSON

(From an Address delivered October 17, 1877.)

BY GEORGE WILLIAM CURTIS

THE drama of the Revolution opened in New England, culminated in New York, and closed in Virginia. It was a happy fortune that the three colonies which represented the various territorial sections of the settled continent were each, in turn, the chief seat of war. The common sacrifice, the common struggle, the common triumph, tended to weld them locally, politically, and morally together. Doubtless there were conflicts of provincial pride and jealousy and suspicion. In every great crisis of war, however, there was a common impulse and devotion, and the welfare of the continent obliterated provincial lines.

It is by the few heaven-piercing peaks, not by the confused mass of upland, that we measure the height of the Andes, of the Alps, of the Himalaya. It is by Joseph Warren not by Benjamin Church, by John Jay not by Sir John Johnson, by George Washington not by Benedict Arnold, that we test the quality of the Revolutionary character. The voice of Patrick Henry from the mountains answered that of James Otis by the sea. Paul Revere's lantern shone along through the valley of the Hudson, and flashed along the cliffs of the Blue Ridge. The scattering volley of Lexington green swelled to the triumphant thunder of Saratoga, and the reverberation of Burgoyne's falling arms in New York shook those of Cornwallis in Virginia from his hands. Doubts, jealousies, prejudices, were merged in one common devotion. The union of the colonies to secure liberty, foretold the union of the States to maintain it, and wherever we stand on Revolutionary fields, or inhale the sweetness of Revolutionary memories, we tread the ground and breathe the air of invincible national union.

So, upon this famous and decisive field, let every unworthy feeling perish! Here, to the England that we fought let us now, grown great and strong with a hundred years, hold out the hand of fellowship and peace! Here, where the English Burgoyne, in the very moment of his bitter humiliation generously pledged George Washington, let us, in our high hour of triumph, of power, and of hope, pledge the queen! Here, in the grave of brave and unknown foemen, may mutual jealousies and doubts and animosities lie buried forever! Henceforth, revering their common glorious traditions, may England, and America press forward side by side, in noble and inspiring rivalry to promote the welfare of man!

Fellow-citizens, with the story of Burgoyne's surrender, the Revolutionary glory of the State of New York, still fresh in our memories, I am glad that the hallowed spot on which we stand compels us to remember not only the imperial State, but the national Commonwealth, whose young hands here together struck the blow, and on whose older head descends the ample benediction of the victory. On yonder height, a hundred years ago, Virginia and Pennsylvania lay encamped. Beyond, and further to the north, watched New Hampshire and Vermont. Here, in the wooded uplands at the south, stood New Jersey and New York, while across the river to the east, Connecticut and Massachusetts closed the triumphant line. Here was the symbol of the Revolution, a common cause, a common strife, a common triumph; the cause, not of a class, but of human nature; the triumph, not of a colony, but of united America.

And we who stand here proudly remembering, we who have seen Virginia and New York, the North and the South, more bitterly hostile than the armies whose battles shook this ground, we who mutually proved in deadlier conflict the constancy and courage of all the States, which, proud to be peers, yet own no master but their united selves, we renew our heart's imperishable devotion to the common American faith, the common American pride, the common American glory! Here America stood and triumphed. Here Americans stand and bless their memory. And here, for a thousand years, many grateful generations of Americans come to rehearse the glorious story, and to rejoice in a supreme and benignant American nationality!

THE SURRENDER OF BURGOYNE

BY JAMES WATTS DE PEYSTER

(Extract from Centennial Poem, read October 17, 1877.)

BROTHERS, this spot is holy! Look around!
  Before us flows our memory's sacred river,
Whose banks are Freedom's shrines. This grassy
    mound,
  The altar, on whose height the Mighty Giver
Gave Independence to our country; when,
Thanks to its brave, enduring, patient men,
The invading host was brought to bay, and laid
Beneath " Old Glory's " new-born folds, the blade,
The brazen thunder-throats, the pomp of War,
And England's yoke, broken forevermore.

   .   .   .   .

Yes, on this spot,— thanks to our gracious God,—
Where last in conscious arrogance it trod,
Defiled, as captives, Burgoyne's conquered horde;
Below, their general yielded up his sword;
There, to our flag bowed England's, battle-torn;
Where now we stand, the United States was born.

THE SARATOGA MONUMENT BEGUN

BY HORATIO SEYMOUR

(From Address delivered October 17, 1877.)

ONE hundred years ago, on this spot, American independence was made a great fact in the history of
nations. Until the surrender of the British army un-

der Burgoyne, the Declaration of Independence was but a declaration. It was a patriotic purpose asserted in bold words by brave men, who pledged for its maintenance their lives, their fortunes, and their sacred honor. But here it was made a fact by virtue of armed force. It had been regarded by the world merely as an act of defiance, but it was now seen that it contained the germs of a government which the event we celebrate made one of the powers of the earth. Here rebellion was made revolution. Upon this ground, that which had in the eye of the law been treason, became triumphant patriotism. At the break of day, in the judgment of the world, our fathers were rebels. When the echoes of the evening gun died away along this valley, they were patriots who had rescued their country from wrong and outrage. We had passed through the baptism of blood, and gained a name among the nations of the earth.

Before the Revolution the people of the several colonies held but little intercourse. They were estranged from each other by distance, by sectional prejudices, by differences of lineage and religious creeds. But when the men of Virginia went to Massachusetts to rescue Boston, when the men of the East and South battled side by side with those from the Middle States, when Greene and Lincoln went to the relief of the Southern colonies, all prejudices not only died away, but more than fraternal love animated every patriotic heart from the bleak forests of New England to the milder airs of Georgia. And now that a hundred years have passed, and our country has become great beyond the wildest dreams of our fathers, will not the story of their sufferings revive in the breast of all the love of our country, of our common country, and all who live within its boundaries?

It was the most remarkable fact of the Revolutionary War and of the formation of state and national governments, that although the colonists were of different lineages and languages, living under different climates, with varied pursuits and forms of labor, cut off from intercourse by distance, yet, in spite of all these obstacles to accord, they were from the outset animated by common views, feelings, and purposes. When the independence was gained, they were able, after a few weeks spent in consultation, to form the constitution under which we have lived for nearly one hundred years. There can be no stronger proof that American institutions were born and shaped by American necessities. This fact should give us new faith in the lasting nature of our government.

Monuments make as well as mark the civilization of a people. The surrender of Burgoyne marks the dividing line between two conditions of our country: the one the colonial period of dependence, and the other the day from which it stood full-armed and victorious here, endowed with a boldness to assert its independence, and endowed with a wisdom to frame its own system of government. We are told that during more than twenty centuries of war and bloodshed, only fifteen battles have been decisive of lasting results. The contest of Saratoga is one of them. Shall not some suitable structure recall this fact to the public mind? Neither France, nor Britain, nor Germany could spare the statues or works of art which keep alive the memory of patriotic services or of personal virtues. Such silent teachers of all that ennobles men, have taught their lessons through the darkest ages, and have done much to save society from sinking into utter decay and degradation. If Greece or Rome had left no memorials of private virtues or public greatness, the progress of civilization would have been slow and feeble. If their crumbling remains should be swept away, the world would mourn the loss, not only to learning and the arts, but to virtue and patriotism. It concerns the honor and welfare of the American people that this spot should be marked by some structure which should recall its history and animate all, who look upon it, by its grand teachings. No people ever held lasting power or greatness who did not reverence the virtues of their fathers, or who did not show forth this reverence by material and striking testimonials.

Let us, then, build here, a lasting monument, which shall tell of our gratitude to those who, through suffering and sacrifice, wrought out the independence of our country.

MOLLY MAGUIRE AT MONMOUTH

(June 28, 1778.)

BY WILLIAM COLLINS

On the bloody field of Monmouth
　　Flashed the guns of Greene and Wayne,
Fiercely roared the tide of battle,
　　Thick the sward was heaped with slain.
Foremost, facing death and danger,
　　Hessian, horse, and grenadier,
In the vanguard, fiercely fighting,
　　Stood an Irish Cannonier.

Loudly roared his iron cannon,
   Mingling ever in the strife,
And beside him, firm and daring,
   Stood his faithful Irish wife.
Of her bold contempt of danger
   Greene and Lee's brigades could tell,
Every one knew " Captain Molly,"
   And the army loved her well.

Surged the roar of battle round them,
   Swiftly flew the iron hail,
Forward dashed a thousand bayonets,
   That lone battery to assail.
From the foeman's foremost columns
   Swept a furious fusillade,
Mowing down the massed battalions
   In the ranks of Greene's Brigade.

Fast and faster worked the gunner,
   Soiled with powder, blood and dust,
English bayonets shone before him,
   Shot and shell around him burst;
Still he fought with reckless daring,
   Stood and manned her long and well,
Till at last the gallant fellow
   Dead — beside his cannon fell.

With a bitter cry of sorrow,
   And a dark and angry frown,
Looked that band of gallant patriots
   At their gunner stricken down.
" Fall back, comrades, it is folly
   Thus to strive against the foe."
" No! not so," cried Irish Molly;
   " We can strike another blow."

Quickly leaped she to the cannon,
   In her fallen husband's place,
Sponged and rammed it fast and steady,
   Fired it in the foeman's face.
Flashed another ringing volley,
   Roared another from the gun;
" Boys, hurrah! " cried gallant Molly,
   " For the flag of Washington."

Greene's Brigade, though shorn and shattered,
   Slain and bleeding half their men,
When they heard that Irish slogan,
   Turned and charged the foe again.
Knox and Wayne and Morgan rally,
   To the front they forward wheel,
And before their rushing onset
   Clinton's English columns reel.

Still the cannon's voice in anger
   Rolled and rattled o'er the plain,
Till there lay in swarms around it
   Mangled heaps of Hessian slain.
" Forward! charge them with the bayonet! "
   'Twas the voice of Washington,
And there burst a fiery greeting
   From the Irish woman's gun.

Monckton falls; against his columns
   Leap the troops of Wayne and Lee,
And before their reeking bayonets
   Clinton's red battalions flee.
Morgan's rifles, fiercely flashing,
   Thin the foe's retreating ranks,
And behind them onward dashing
   Ogden hovers on their flanks.

Fast they fly, these boasting Britons,
    Who in all their glory came,
With their brutal Hessian hirelings
    To wipe out our country's name.
Proudly floats the starry banner,
    Monmouth's glorious field is won,
And in triumph Irish Molly,
    Stands beside her smoking gun.

THE SOUTH IN THE REVOLUTION

BY ROBERT YOUNG HAYNE

IF there be one State in the Union, and I say it not in a boasting spirit, that may challenge comparison with any other, for an uniform, zealous, ardent, and uncalculating devotion to the Union, that State is South Carolina.

From the very commencement of the Revolution, up to this hour, there is no sacrifice, however great, she has not cheerfully made, no service she has even hesitated to perform. She has adhered to you, in your prosperity; but in your adversity she has clung to you with more than filial affection. No matter what was the condition of her domestic affairs, though deprived of her resources, divided by parties, or surrounded by difficulties, the call of the country has been to her as the voice of God. Domestic discord ceased at the sound; every man became at once reconciled to his brethren, and the sons of Carolina were all seen crowding together to the temple, bringing their gifts to the altar of their common country.

What was the conduct of the South during the

Revolution? I honor New England for her conduct in that glorious struggle. But, great as is the praise which belongs to her, I think at least equal honor is due to the South. They espoused the quarrel of their brethren with a generous zeal which did not suffer them to stop to calculate their interest in the dispute. Favorites of the mother-country, possessed of neither ships nor seamen to create a commercial rivalship, they might have found, in their situation, a guarantee that their trade would be forever fostered and protected by Great Britain. But, trampling on all considerations, either of interest or of safety, they rushed into the conflict; and, fighting for principle, periled all in the sacred cause of freedom. Never was there exhibited in the history of the world higher examples of noble daring, dreadful suffering, and heroic endurance than by the Whigs of Carolina during the Revolution! The whole state, from the mountains to the sea, was overrun by an overwhelming force of the enemy. The fruits of industry perished on the spot where they were produced, or were consumed by the foe. The " Plains of Carolina " drank up the most precious blood of her citizens. Black and smoking ruins marked the places which had been the habitations of her children. Driven from their homes, into the gloomy and almost impenetrable swamps, even there the spirit of liberty survived, and South Carolina, sustained by the example of her Sumters and her Marions, proved, by her conduct, that, though her soil might be overrun, the spirit of her people was invincible.

THE SONG OF MARION'S MEN

(1780–1781.)

BY WILLIAM CULLEN BRYANT

While the British Army held South Carolina, Marion and Sumter gathered bands of partisans and waged a vigorous guerilla warfare most harassing and destructive to the invader.

OUR band is few, but true and tried,
    Our leader frank and bold;
The British soldier trembles
    When Marion's name is told.
Our fortress is the good greenwood
    Our tent the cypress-tree;
We know the forest round us,
    As seamen know the sea.
We know its walls of thorny vines,
    Its glades of reedy grass,
Its safe and silent islands
    Within the dark morass.

Wo to the English soldiery,
    That little dread us near!
On them shall light at midnight
    A strange and sudden fear:
When, waking to their tents on fire
    They grasp their arms in vain,
And they who stand to face us
    Are beat to earth again.

And they who fly in terror deem
  A mighty host behind,
And hear the tramp of thousands
  Upon the hollow wind.

Then sweet the hour that brings release
  From danger and from toil;
We talk the battle over,
  And share the battle's spoil.
The woodland rings with laugh and shout,
  As if a hunt were up,
And woodland flowers are gathered
  To crown the soldier's cup.
With merry songs we mock the wind
  That in the pine-top grieves,
And slumber long and sweetly
  On beds of oaken leaves.

Well knows the fair and friendly moon
  The band that Marion leads —
The glitter of their rifles,
  The scampering of their steeds.
'Tis life to guide the fiery barb
  Across the moonlight plain;
'Tis life to feel the night-wind
  That lifts his tossing mane.
A moment in the British camp —
  A moment — and away
Back to the pathless forest,
  Before the peep of day.

Grave men there are by broad Santee,
  Grave men with hoary hairs;
Their hearts are all with Marion,
  For Marion are their prayers.

And lovely ladies greet our band
With kindliest welcoming,
With smiles like those of summer,
And tears like those of spring.
For them we wear these trusty arms,
And lay them down no more
Till we have driven down the Briton,
Forever, from our shore.

OUR COUNTRY SAVED

BY JAMES RUSSELL LOWELL

(Extract from Ode recited at the Harvard Commemoration, July 21, 1865.)

BOOM, cannon, boom to all the winds and waves!
Clash out, glad bells, from every rocking steeple!
Banners, advance with triumph, bend your staves!
And from every mountain-peak
Let beacon-fire to answering beacon speak,
Katahdin tell Monadnock, Whiteface he,
And so leap on in light from sea to sea,
Till the glad news be sent
Across a kindling continent,
Making earth feel more firm and air breathe braver:
Be proud! for she is saved, and all have helped to save
    her!
She that lifts up the manhood of the poor,
She of the open soul and open door,
With room about her hearth for all mankind!
The fire is dreadful in her eyes no more;
From her bold front the helm she doth unbind,
Sends all her handmaid armies back to spin,

And bids her navies, that so lately hurled
Their crashing battle, to hold their thunders in,
Swimming like birds of calm along the unharmful
    shore.
No challenge sends she to the older world,
That looked askance and hatred; a light scorn
Plays o'er her mouth, as round her mighty knees
She calls her children back, and waits the morn
Of nobler days, enthroned between her subject seas.

Bow down, dear land, for thou hast found release!
Thy God, in these distempered days,
Hath taught thee the sure wisdom of His ways,
And through thine enemies hath wrought thee peace!
Bow down in prayer and praise!
No poorest in thy borders but may now
Lift to the juster skies a man's enfranchised brow.
O Beautiful! my Country! ours once more!
Smoothing thy gold of war-disheveled hair
O'er such sweet brows as never other wore,
    And letting thy set lips
    Freed from wrath's pale eclipse,
The rosy edges of their smile lay bare;
What words divine of lover or of poet
Could tell our love and make thee know it,
Among the nations bright beyond compare?
    What were our lives without thee?
    What all our lives to save thee?
    We reck not what we gave thee;
    We will not dare to doubt thee,
But ask whatever else, and we will dare!

NEW ENGLAND AND VIRGINIA

BY ROBERT CHARLES WINTHROP

THERE are circumstances of peculiar and beautiful correspondence in the careers of Virginia and New England which must ever constitute a bond of sympathy, affection, and pride between their children. Not only did they form respectively the great northern and southern rallying points of civilization on this continent; not only was the most friendly competition or the most cordial coöperation, as circumstances allowed, kept up between them during their early colonial existence — but who forgets the generous emulation, the noble rivalry, with which they continually challenged and seconded each other in resisting the first beginnings of British aggression, in the persons of their James Otises and Patrick Henrys?

Who forgets that while that resistance was first brought to a practical test in New England, at Lexington and Concord and Bunker Hill, Fortune reserved for Yorktown of Virginia the last crowning battle of Independence? Who forgets that while the hand by which the original Declaration of Independence was drafted, was furnished by Virginia, the tongue by which the adoption of that instrument was defended and secured, was furnished by New England,— a bond of common glory, upon which not Death alone seemed to set his seal, but Deity, I had almost said, to affix an immortal sanction, when the spirits by which that hand and voice were moved, were caught up together to the clouds on the same great Day of the Nation's Jubilee.

VI
SWEET LAND OF LIBERTY

AMERICA [1]

BY S. F. SMITH

My country, 'tis of Thee,
Sweet Land of Liberty
Of thee I sing;
Land where my fathers died,
Land of the pilgrims' pride,
From every mountain side
Let Freedom ring.

My native country, thee,
Land of the noble free,
Thy name I love;
I love thy rocks and rills,
Thy woods and templed hills,
My heart with rapture thrills
Like that above.

[1] *The origin of the words of the patriotic hymn, " America," has been somewhat recently celebrated by an anniversary.
The air, as is well known, is that of the national anthem of
England, " God Save the King." As such it has been in use,
in one form or another, since the middle of the last century.
In 1832, Dr. S. F. Smith came upon it in a " book of German music," and on the spur of the moment, as it appears,
wrote for it the hymn " America." This was in Andover,
Mass., in February, 1832. The hymn was first sung publicly
at a children's celebration at the Park Street Church, Boston,
on July 4th of that year.*
*" If I had anticipated the future of it, doubtless, I should
have taken more pains with it," wrote Doctor Smith, in 1872.
" Such as it is, I am glad to have contributed this mite to
the cause of American freedom."*

Let music swell the breeze,
And ring from all the trees
 Sweet Freedom's song;
Let mortal tongues awake;
Let all that breathe partake;
Let rocks their silence break,
 The sound prolong.

Our fathers' God to Thee,
Author of Liberty,
 To thee we sing,
Long may our land be bright
With Freedom's holy light,
Protect us by thy might
 Great God, our King.

Our glorious Land to-day,
'Neath Education's sway,
 Soars upward still.
Its halls of learning fair,
Whose bounties all may share,
Behold them everywhere
 On vale and hill!

Thy safeguard, Liberty,
The school shall ever be,—
 Our Nation's pride!
No tyrant hand shall smite,
While with encircling might
All here are taught the Right
 With Truth allied.

Beneath Heaven's gracious will
The stars of progress still
    Our course do sway;
In unity sublime
To broader heights we climb,
Triumphant over Time,
    God speeds our way!

Grand birthright of our sires,
Our altars and our fires
    Keep we still pure!
Our starry flag unfurled,
The hope of all the world,
In Peace and Light impearled,
    God hold secure!

THE REPUBLIC

(From " The Building of the Ship.")

BY HENRY WADSWORTH LONGFELLOW

THOU, too, sail on, O Ship of State!
Sail on, O UNION, strong and great!
Humanity with all its fears,
With all the hopes of future years,
Is hanging breathless on thy fate!
We know what Master laid thy keel,
What Workmen wrought thy ribs of steel,
Who made each mast, and sail, and rope,
What anvils rang, what hammers beat,
In what a forge and what a heat
Were shaped the anchors of thy hope!

Fear not each sudden sound and shock,
'Tis of the wave and not the rock;
'Tis but the flapping of the sail,
And not a rent made by the gale!
In spite of rock and tempest's roar,
In spite of false lights on the shore,
Sail on, nor fear to breast the sea!
Our hearts, our hopes, are all with thee,
Our hearts, our hopes, our prayers, our tears,
Our faith triumphant o'er our fears,
Are all with thee,— are all with thee!

THE ANTIQUITY OF FREEDOM

BY WILLIAM CULLEN BRYANT

HERE are old trees, tall oaks, and gnarlèd pines,
That stream with gray-green mosses; here the ground
Was never trenched by spade, and flowers spring up
Unsown, and die ungathered.   It is sweet
To linger here, among the flitting birds
And leaping squirrels, wandering brooks, and winds
That shake the leaves, and scatter, as they pass,
A fragrance from the cedars, thickly set
With pale blue berries.   In these peaceful shades —
Peaceful, unpruned, immeasurably old —
My thoughts go up the long dim path of years,
Back to the earliest days of liberty.

O Freedom! thou art not, as poets dream,
A fair young girl, with light and delicate limbs,
And wavy tresses gushing from the cap
With which the Roman master crowned his slave

When he took off the gyves. A bearded man,
Armed to the teeth, art thou; one mailèd hand
Grasps the broad shield, and one the sword; thy brow,
Glorious in beauty though it be, is scarred
With tokens of old wars; thy massive limbs
Are strong with struggling. Power at thee has launched
His bolts, and with his lightnings smitten thee;
They could not quench the life thou hast from heaven;
Merciless Power has dug thy dungeon deep,
And his swart armorers, by a thousand fires,
Have forged thy chain; yet, while he deems thee bound,
The links are shivered, and the prison walls
Fall outward; terribly thou springest forth,
As springs the flame above a burning pile,
And shoutest to the nations, who return
Thy shoutings, while the pale oppressor flies.

Thy birthright was not given by human hands:
Thou wert twin-born with man. In pleasant fields,
While yet our race was few, thou sat'st with him,
To tend the quiet flock and watch the stars,
And teach the reed to utter simple airs.
Thou by his side, amid the tangled wood,
Didst war upon the panther and the wolf,
His only foes; and thou with him didst draw
The earliest furrow on the mountain's side,
Soft with the deluge. Tyranny himself,
Thy enemy, although of reverend look,
Hoary with many years, and far obeyed,
Is later born than thou; and as he meets
The grave defiance of thine elder eye,
The usurper trembles in his fastnesses.

Thou shalt wax stronger with the lapse of years,
But he shall fade into a feebler age —
Feebler, yet subtler. He shall weave his snares,
And spring them on thy careless steps, and clap
His withered hands, and from their ambush call
His hordes to fall upon thee. He shall send
Quaint maskers, wearing fair and gallant forms
To catch thy gaze, and uttering graceful words
To charm they ear; while his sly imps, by stealth,
Twine round thee threads of steel, light thread on
        thread,
That grow to fetters; or bind down thy arms
With chains concealed in chaplets. Oh! not yet
Mayst thou unbrace thy corselet, nor lay by
Thy sword; nor yet, O Freedom! close thy lids
In slumber; for thine enemy never sleeps,
And thou must watch and combat till the day
Of the new earth and heaven.

AMERICA

BY WILLIAM CULLEN BRYANT

OH, mother of a mighty race,
Yet lovely in thy youthful grace!
The elder dames, thy haughty peers,
Admire and hate thy blooming years.
            With words of shame
And taunts of scorn they join thy name.

For on thy cheeks the glow is spread
That tints thy morning hills with red;

Thy step — the wild deer's rustling feet
Within thy woods are not more fleet;
    Thy hopeful eye
Is bright as thine own sunny sky.

Aye, let them rail — those haughty ones,
While safe thou dwellest with thy sons.
They do not know how loved thou art,
How many a fond and fearless heart
    Would rise to throw
Its life between thee and the foe.

They know not, in their hate and pride,
What virtues with thy children bide;
How true, how good, thy graceful maids
Make bright, like flowers, the valley shades;
    What generous men
Spring, like thine oaks, by hill and glen; —

What cordial welcomes greet the guest
By thy lone rivers of the West;
How faith is kept, and truth revered,
And man is loved, and God is feared,
    In woodland homes,
And where the ocean border foams.

There's freedom at thy gates and rest
For Earth's down-trodden and opprest,
A shelter for the hunted head,
For the starved laborer toil and bread.
    Power, at thy bounds,
Stops and calls back his baffled hounds.

Oh, fair young mother! on thy brow
Shall sit a nobler grace than now.
Deep in the brightness of the skies
The thronging years in glory rise,
    And, as they fleet,
Drop strength and riches at thy feet.

Thine eye, with every coming hour,
Shall brighten, and thy form shall tower;
And when thy sisters, elder born,
Would brand thy name with words of scorn,
    Before thine eye,
Upon their lips the taunt shall die.

ODE

BY RALPH WALDO EMERSON

(Sung in the Town Hall, Concord, July 4, 1857.)

O TENDERLY the haughty day
  Fills his blue urn with fire;
One morn is in the mighty heaven,
  And one in our desire.

The cannon booms from town to town,
  Our pulses beat not less,
The joy-bells chime their tidings down,
  Which children's voices bless.

For He that flung the broad blue fold
  O'er-mantling land and sea,
One third part of the sky unrolled
  For the banner of the free.

The men are ripe of Saxon kind
　To build an equal state,—
To take the statute from the mind
　And make of duty fate.

United States! the ages plead,—
　Present and Past in under-song,—
Go put your creed into your deed,
　Nor speak with double tongue.

For sea and land don't understand
　Nor skies without a frown
See rights for which the one hand fights
　By the other cloven down.

Be just at home; then write your scroll
　Of honor o'er the sea,
And bid the broad Atlantic roll
　A ferry of the free.

And henceforth there shall be no chain,
　Save underneath the sea
The wires shall murmur through the main
　Sweet songs of liberty.

The conscious stars accord above,
　The waters wild below,
And under, through the cable wove,
　Her fiery errands go.

AMERICA FIRST [1]

'ANONYMOUS

THIS is the season when Young America celebrates the glorious deeds of the forefathers, when they cut the leading-strings that bound them to the Old World, and stepped forth with the independence of manhood.

It took Rome five hundred years, five centuries of war, intrigue and arrogance, to overspread Southern Europe. In a little more than one century America has grown to a magnitude in area and perhaps in population also, equal to that of Rome in its most magnificent days.

" *Civis Romanus sum!* " was the proudest boast that could fall from the lips of man at the beginning of the Christian era. Is there to-day an American who rates his citizenship in the Great Republic at a lower value than Roman freedom nineteen hundred years ago?

The day for " spread-eagle " brag is long past, but there is no reason why we should hesitate to say what not we alone but all the people of the world believe, that it is the destiny of this country to become the greatest, the strongest, the wealthiest, the most self-supporting of all the nations of the earth. It is already the greatest self-governing community the world has ever seen.

How can we make it greater? By standing together as Americans. We shall not magnify, but shall belittle ourselves, if we swagger before our neighbors — using bravado for the strong, and insolence in

[1] *From " The Youth's Companion."*

our treatment of the weak. But we should take American views instead of party views, when questions arise between this government and others.

The motto " America against the world " would be a contemptible motto. Yet is it not better to adopt even such a motto than to take the side of the world against America, or to be indifferent when the interests of one's own country are assailed?

The Fourth of July is a good time for us all to resolve that we will be Americans at heart. Not that we will build up our own country on the ruins of others, but that when there is a clashing of interests those of our native land shall have our hearty support.

LIBERTY FOR ALL

BY WILLIAM LLOYD GARRISON

THEY tell me, Liberty! that in thy name
I may not plead for all the human race;
That some are born to bondage and disgrace,
Some to a heritage of woe and shame,
And some to power supreme, and glorious fame:
With my whole soul I spurn the doctrine base,
And, as an equal brotherhood, embrace
All people, and for all fair freedom claim!
Know this, O man! whate'er thy earthly fate —
God never made a tyrant nor a slave:
Woe, then, to those who dare to desecrate
His glorious image! — for to all He gave
Eternal rights, which none may violate;
And, by a mighty hand, the oppressed He yet shall
save!

HYMN

(For the Fourth of July, 1863.)

ANONYMOUS

LORD, the people of the land
In Thy presence humbly stand;
On this day, when Thou didst free
Men of old from tyranny,
We, their children, bow to Thee.
  Help us, Lord, our only trust!
  We are helpless, we are dust!

All our homes are red with blood;
Long our grief we have withstood;
Every lintel, each door-post,
Drips, at tidings from the host,
With the blood of some one lost.
  Help us, Lord, our only trust!
  We are helpless, we are dust!

Comfort, Lord, the grieving one
Who bewails a stricken son!
Comfort, Lord, the weeping wife,
In her long, long widowed life,
Brooding o'er the fatal strife,
  Help us, Lord, our only trust!
  We are helpless, we are dust!

On our Nation's day of birth,
Bless Thy own long-favored earth!

Urge the soldier with Thy will!
Aid their leaders with Thy skill!
Let them hear Thy trumpet thrill!
  Help us, Lord, our only trust!
  We are helpless, we are dust!

Lord, we only fight for peace,
Fight that freedom may increase.
Give us back the peace of old,
When the land with plenty rolled,
And our banner awed the bold!
  Help us, Lord, our only trust!
  We are helpless, we are dust!

Lest we pray in thoughtless guilt,
Shape the future as Thou wilt!
Purge our realm from hoary crime
With Thy battles, dread, sublime,
In Thy well-appointed time!
  Help us, Lord, our only trust!
  We are helpless, we are dust!

With one heart the Nation's cries
From our choral lips arise:
Thou didst point a noble way
For our Fathers through the fray;
Lead their children thus to-day!
  Help us, Lord, our only trust!
  We are helpless, we are dust!

In His name, who bravely bore
Cross and crown begemmed with gore,

By His last immortal groan,
Ere He mounted to His throne,
Make our sacred cause Thy own!
Help us, Lord, our only trust!
We are helpless, we are dust!

THE DAWNING FUTURE

BY WILLIAM PRESTON JOHNSON, PRESIDENT OF
TULANE UNIVERSITY, LA.

(Closing stanza of patriotic poem, "The Patriot South.")

THUS, in the march of time, and long procession
Of coming ages, year on year,
We mark the great Republic's proud career,
Like Philip's phalanx, manifold,
With bucklers linked, one front against aggression,
Till Freedom's perfect vision is unrolled,
And man, with eye unsealed, its glories shall behold.

LIBERTY

THE people never give up their liberties but under
some delusion.
BURKE — *Speech at a County Meeting at Bucks,* 1784.

Liberty's in every blow!
Let us do or die.
BURNS — *Bannockburn.*

What is liberty without wisdom and without virtue?
It is the greatest of all possible evils; for it is folly,
vice, and madness, without tuition or restraint.
BURKE — *Reflections on the Revolution in France.*

The poorest man may in his cottage bid defiance to
all the force of the crown.
  EARL OF CHATHAM — *Speech on the Excise Bill.*

'Tis liberty alone that gives the flower
Of fleeting life its luster and perfume;
And we are weeds without it.
  COWPER — *The Task.* Bk. V. Line 446.

The love of liberty with life is given,
And life itself the inferior gift of heaven.
DRYDEN — *Palamon and Arcite.* Bk. II. Line 291.

This is true liberty when freeborn men,
Having to advise the public, may speak free:
Which he who can and will deserves high praise:
Who neither can nor will may hold his peace.
What can be juster in a state than this?
  MILTON — Trans. *Horace.* Ep. i. 16, 40.

Give me again my hollow tree
A crust of bread, and liberty!
POPE — *Imitations of Horace.* Bk. II. Satire VI.
  Line 220.

O Liberty! Liberty! how many crimes are com-
mitted in thy name!
  MADAME ROLAND — *Macaulay. Mirabeau.*

FREEDOM

HEREDITARY bondsmen! Know ye not
Who would be free themselves must strike the blow?
  BYRON — *Childe Harold.* Canto II. St. 67.

Freedom has a thousand charms to show,
That slaves howe'er contented, never know.
>   Cowper — *Table Talk.*   Line 260.

He is the freeman, whom the truth makes free,
And all are slaves besides.
>   Cowper — *The Task.*   Bk. V.   Line 733.

When Freedom from her mountain height
    Unfurled her standard to the air,
She tore the azure robe of night,
    And set the stars of glory there.
>   Drake — *The American Flag.*

My angel — his name is Freedom,—
Choose him to be your king;
He shall cut pathways east and west,
And fend you with his wing.
>   Emerson — *Boston Hymn.*

Yes, to this thought I hold with firm persistence;
The last result of wisdom stamps it true;
He only earns his freedom and existence
Who daily conquers them anew.
>   Goethe — *Faust.*

Know ye why the Cypress tree as Freedom's tree is
    known?
Know ye why the Lily fair as Freedom's flower is
    shown?
Hundred arms the Cypress has, yet never plunder
    seeks;
With ten well-developed tongues the Lily never
    speaks!
>   Omar Khayyam — Frederich Boden-
>   stedt, Translator.

What is freedom?   Rightly understood,
A universal license to be good.
                    HARTLEY COLERIDGE.

A RHAPSODY

BY CASSIUS MARCELLUS CLAY

I MAY be an enthusiast; but I cannot but give utterance to the conceptions of my own mind. When I look upon the special developments of European civilization; when I contemplate the growing freedom of the cities, and the middle class which has sprung up between the pretenders to divine rule on the one hand, and the abject serf on the other; when I consider the Reformation, and the invention of the press, and see, on the southern shore of the continent, an humble individual, amidst untold difficulties and repeated defeats, pursuing the mysterious suggestions which the mighty deep poured unceasingly upon his troubled spirit, till at last, with great and irrepressible energy of soul, he discovered that there lay in the far western ocean a continent open for the infusion of those elementary principles of liberty which were dwarfed in European soil,— I conceive that the hand of destiny was there!

When I see the immigration of the Pilgrims from the chalky shores of England,— in the night fleeing from their native home,— so dramatically and ably pictured by Mr. Webster in his celebrated oration,— when father, mother, brother, wife, sister, lover, were all lost by those melancholy wanderers —" stifling," in the language of one who is immortal in the con-

ception, "the mighty hunger of the heart," and land-
ing, amidst cold and poverty and death, upon the rude
rocks of Plymouth,— I venture to think the will of
Deity was there!

When I have remembered the Revolution of '76,—
the Seven Years' War — three millions of men in
arms against the most powerful nation in history, and
vindicating their independence,— I have thought that
their sufferings and death were not in vain! When
I have seen the forsaken hearthstone,— looked upon
the battlefield, upon the dying and the dead,— heard
the agonizing cry, "Water, for the sake of God!
water;" seeing the dissolution of being — pale lips
pressing in death the yet loved images of wife, sister,
lover,— I have not deemed — I will not deem all
these things in vain! I cannot regard this great continent, reaching from the Atlantic to the far Pacific,
and from the St. John's to the Rio del Norte, as the
destined home of a barbarian people of third-rate
civilization.

Like the Roman who looked back upon the glory of
his ancestors, in woe, exclaiming,

"Great Scipio's ghost complains that we are slow,
And Pompey's shade walks unavenged among us,"

the great dead hover around me: — Lawrence, "Don't
give up the ship."— Henry, "Give me liberty or give
me death!"— Adams, "Survive or perish, I am for
the Declaration."— Allan, "In the name of the living
God, I come!"

Come then, Thou Eternal, who dwellest not in
temples made with hands, but who, in the city's crowd
or by the far forest stream, revealest Thyself to the

earnest seeker after the true and right, inspire my
heart; give me undying courage to pursue the prompt-
ings of my spirit; and whether I shall be called in the
shades of life to look upon as sweet and kind and
lovely faces as now, or shut in by sorrow and night,
horrid visions shall gloom upon me in my dying hour,
O my country, mayest thou yet be free!

COLUMBIA

BY FREDERICK LAWRENCE KNOWLES

MATED to the Millennium,— Time's last heir
    And proudest daughter, conquerless as he;
Girdled with lakes like jewels princely fair,
    With strong feet planted in the Mexic sea!

Where Law is liberty, where Love is power,
    And the twain one, there Treason cannot dwell;
A fangless asp, it coiled one impotent hour,
    But at thy white glance backward writhed to hell.

Leave dotard empires flames of drunken war,
    Be thine chaste hours of labor and increase,
Vineyards and harvests yielding guiltless store,
    Toil's bloodless battles on the plains of peace!

Yet when slain Weakness, dying at thy door,
    Summoning thy right arm's vengeance, clasps thy
        feet,—
Thy sword that drinks her murderer's blood is pure
    As laughing sickles in the saffron wheat.

Clearing a crimson path where Peace may tread
  More safely; thou dost play thy patient part,
Love's pledged ally,— yea, though thy blade be red;
  Thrusting War's weapons thro' his own false heart.

O goddess, arctic-crowned and tropic-shod
  And belted with great waters, hear our cry,—
More honest never reached the ear of God,—
  We'll serve thee, laud thee, love thee, till we die!

A RENAISSANCE OF PATRIOTISM [1]

BY GEORGE J. MANSON

A RENAISSANCE

WITHIN the past few years there has been what ex-President Harrison once happily termed "a renaissance of patriotism." It started with the centennial anniversaries of 1776, which had the effect of carrying the memories of the people back to the period of the Nation's birth, and subsequently resulted in the formation of several societies which will be the means of fostering the patriotic spirit and love of country, and recall remembrances of our Revolutionary struggle. The organizers of these societies found that there was a growing lack of what may be called national patriotism — the patriotism that grows out of a lively recollection of the early making of the country through battle, toil, and hardship of the fathers. This lukewarm spirit was not charged to the flood of immigration, or to the lapse of time, but was principally due

[1] *Reprinted from " The Independent."*

to neglect on the part of the descendants of Revolutionary heroes to perform their duty of keeping before the public mind the memory of the services of their ancestors, the times in which they lived and the principles for which they contended.

THE SONS OF THE REVOLUTION

One of the first of these societies to be started was the " Sons of the Revolution." This was organized February 22, 1876, reorganized December 4, 1883, and incorporated May 3, 1884. The aim of this society is to perpetuate the memory of the men who, in military, naval or civil service, by their acts or counsel, achieved American independence. The members promote and assist in the proper celebration of the anniversaries of Washington's Birthday, the battles of Lexington and Bunker Hill, the Fourth of July, the capitulation of Saratoga and Yorktown, and the formal evacuation of New York by the British army, December 3, 1783, as a relinquishment of territorial sovereignty, and other prominent events relating to or connected with the War of the Revolution.

The roll-book of the members is something more than a mere list of names. Before each name is the year, showing when the member was admitted into the society, and there is also given in a paragraph his genealogical history so far as it relates to his ancestors who were in any way connected with the Revolutionary struggle. There is a general, or national society, divided into state societies which regulate their own affairs. Under the rules of the New York State society, ten or more members can organize within any county outside of the county of New York, such a

body being called a local chapter. The total membership is now about six thousand. When membership
is asked on the ground of an ancestor having been
a " sailor " or " marine," it must be shown that such
service was other than shore duty and regularly performed in the Continental navy, or the navy of one
of the original thirteen states, or on an armed vessel
other than a merchant ship. When the ancestor has
been an " official " his service must have been suf-
ficiently important in character to have rendered him
specially liable to arrest and imprisonment, if captured
by the enemy, as well as liable to conviction of treason
against the Government of Great Britain.

A few years ago the society stimulated interest in
its work by offering two prizes to the cadets of the
United States Naval Academy, at Annapolis, Md.,— a
gold medal and a silver medal — for the best original
essays upon the subject, " The Navy of the Revolution." · A singular and patriotic feature of these essays was that they were not to contain less than 1,776
words. A gold medal is likewise annually awarded
by the New York society to a student in the College
of the City of New York, for the best essay on a
patriotic subject, and gold, silver, and bronze medals
to the scholars of the high schools throughout the State
for like essays. Similar prizes are awarded by the
societies in other states.

Congress has also been urged, by the Sons of the
Revolution as a body, to pass a bill which has already
been introduced in that body, making an appropriation of a sum of money to erect a monument to John
Paul Jones. It has also memorialized Congress to
enact such a law as will secure the publication of all
the archives of the United States Government relating

to the War of the Revolution, in a manner similar to the publication of the records of the War of the Rebellion.

The seal of the society is an interesting study, suggesting as it does, in small compass, the spirit of patriotism the society desires to cultivate. The seal consists of the figure of a minuteman, in Continental uniform standing on a ladder leading to a belfry. In his right hand he holds a musket and an olive branch, while his left hand grasps a bell-rope. Above is seen the cracked Liberty bell, from which issues a ribbon bearing the motto of the society: *Exegi monumentum aere perennius.* Many members of this society did gallant service in the war with Spain.

SONS OF THE AMERICAN REVOLUTION

The second important patriotic society is the " Sons of the American Revolution," a name very similar to that of the organization just mentioned. The first branch of this society was formed in California in 1876 by a body of descendants of officers, soldiers, and seamen of the Revolution gathered in San Francisco for the purpose of celebrating the one hundredth anniversary of the Declaration of Independence. Similar societies were therefore organized in other states and, on April 30, 1889, these societies with two or three exceptions celebrated the centennial inauguration of Washington as first President of the United States. This meeting was held in Fraunce's Tavern, in New York City, in the identical long room (now marked with a commemorative tablet) in which Washington bade farewell to his officers, December 3,

1783. The national organization was formed on the occasion of this meeting.

This society exists in about thirty states, and numbers about five thousand members. A singular and interesting feature in connection with this and kindred organizations is that their existence has led to and greatly stimulated genealogical research, a species of investigation to which Americans, as a rule, have given but little attention. Persons who have become interested in these societies, it has been found, have rescued unrecorded facts from the aged members of their families who were destined soon to pass away, information which could have been obtained in no other way and which would have been lost forever in a few years.

The " Sons of the American Revolution " prides itself on being a practical and not merely a sentimental and ornamental organization. It has been particularly active in saving throughout the country valuable historical landmarks, such as the headquarters of Jonathan Trumbull, in Connecticut, which has been obtained and is now used for a museum. It is marking historical spots and, directly and indirectly, securing the erection of memorials of the Revolutionary heroes, such as the Bennington Monument, near that famous battle-field, the statue of Gen. John Stark, in New Hampshire, and a monument to be erected in Baltimore to Maryland's heroes of the Revolution. It has obtained from Congress a law providing for the collection and indexing of the records of service of the Revolution. It has stimulated the general observance of national patriotic holidays, and was influential in setting apart June 14th as " Flag Day " in commemoration of the adoption of the Stars and Stripes as the national standard.

THE SOCIETY OF COLONIAL WARS

" The Society of Colonial Wars," originated in New York, and was instituted August 18, 1892, and incorporated October 18, 1892. In May, 1893, the New York society with the societies in the states of Pennsylvania, Maryland, Massachusetts, Connecticut, and the District of Columbia organized the general society, these states, having been previously chartered by the society in the State of New York. The objects of the organizations are similar to those of the previously named societies, from which they differ only in minor details. The present membership is approximately 3,000. On June 14th of this year (1898) this society joined with the Sons of the Revolution in appropriate ceremonies attending the unveiling of commemorative tablets at Fort Ticonderoga, intended to perpetuate the memories of the capture of the fort by Colonel Ethan Allen and his gallant band, the Colonial battles fought in the vicinity of Fort Ticonderoga, etc.

THE MILITARY ORDER OF FOREIGN WARS

" The Military Order of Foreign Wars " is, as its name implies, a military organization with patriotic objects, having for its scope the period of American history since national independence. The principal feature of the order is the perpetuating of the names, as well as the services, of commissioned officers who served in either the War of the Revolution, the War with Tripoli, the War of 1812, the Mexican War, or the War with Spain. Veteran Companionship, is conferred upon such officers, and Hereditary Companionship upon their direct lineal descendants in the male line. The present membership is 1,400, which is rapidly growing. Other societies that merit more extended notice but which can here only be named are the " Order of Cincinnati," the " Society of the War of 1812," the " Aztec Club," the " Loyal Legion," the " Grand Army of the Republic," the " Flag Association," " Colonial Order of the Acorn," " Order of Washington," the " Pilgrim Society," and some others.

THE DAUGHTERS OF THE REVOLUTION

It is quite natural that women, whose patriotic services during the late Civil War have often been the subject of grateful eulogy, should become interested in this new movement. There are several patriotic societies, composed exclusively of women, the objects of which are practically the same as the organizations which have just been mentioned. The society known as the " Daughters of the Revolution " was organized by Mrs. Flora Adams Darling, September 9, 1891. In October, 1890, was organized the more important society known as the " Daughters of the American Revolution," which now has a membership of about 3,500. This society has state chapters existing in most of the states. To become a member of this society a woman must be not less than eighteen years of age, and be the descendant of an ancestor who loyally rendered material aid as a soldier, sailor or civil officer to the cause of independence. The Daughters of the American Revolution have presented to the City of Paris an equestrian statue of Lafayette designed

and executed by Daniel C. French. It was intended
to be a return of the compliment to the American
people conveyed by the French Government when it
presented to the United States the statue of Washington which is now at the National Capital. The unveiling took place with imposing ceremonies on July
3rd.

THE COLONIAL DAMES OF AMERICA

The "Colonial Dames of America," an organization incorporated in 1893, requires of a member that
she shall be descended in her own right from some ancestor of worthy life who came to reside in the
American colony prior to 1750. This ancestor, or
some one of his descendants, shall be a lineal ascendant of the applicant, and shall have rendered efficient
service to his country during the colonial period
either in the founding of the commonwealth, or of
an institution which has survived and developed into
importance, or who shall have held an important position in the Colonial Government and by distinguished
services shall have contributed to the founding of the
Nation. Services rendered after 1783 are not recognized.

UNITED STATES DAUGHTERS, 1776–1812

Still another woman's patriotic organization is
known as the "United States Daughters, 1776–1812."
This society was founded by Mrs. Flora Adams Darling, and incorporated in 1892. Ladies to be eligible
must be lineal descendants of an ancestor who assisted
in the wars of 1776–1812, either as a military or naval
officer, soldier, sailor, or in any way gave aid to the
cause, tho' the society reserves to itself the privilege

of rejecting any nomination that may not be acceptable to it.

Another patriotic woman's organization tho' not of recent date, which has for years rendered important service, is the "Mount Vernon Ladies' Association," of Washington, D. C. This association has under its care and direction the Washington estate at Mount Vernon, Va. In 1895 a volume entitled "Ancestry" was published by Bailey, Banks and Biddle (Philadelphia) in connection with their Department of Heraldry that contained a complete list of the various patriotic societies, then forty-seven in number. Since the publication of this volume many new societies have sprung up.

CENTENNIAL POEMS

CENTENNIAL HYMN [1]

BY JOHN GREENLEAF WHITTIER

SUNG AT THE OPENING OF THE WORLD'S FAIR AT
PHILADELPHIA, IN 1876.

Our fathers' God, from out whose hand
The centuries fall like grains of sand,
We meet to-day, united, free,
And loyal to our land and Thee,
To thank Thee for the era done,
And trust Thee for the opening one.

[1] *By permission of the publishers, Houghton, Mifflin Co.*

Here, where of old, by Thy design,
The fathers spake that word of Thine
Whose echo is the glad refrain
Of rended bolt and falling chain,—
To grace our festal time, from all
The zones of earth, our guests we call.

Be with us while the New World greets
The Old World, thronging all our streets,
Unveiling all the triumphs won
By art or toil, beneath the sun,
And unto common good ordain
This rivalship of hand and brain.

Thou, who hast here, in Concord, furled
The war-flags of a gathered world,—
Beneath our Western skies fulfill
The Orient's mission of good will,
And, freighted with Love's Golden Fleece,
Send back the Argonauts of Peace.

For Art and Labor, met in truce,
For Beauty made the bride of Use,
We thank Thee; while, withal, we crave
The austere virtues, strong to save,—
The Honor, proof to place or gold,
The Manhood, never bought nor sold.

Oh, make Thou us, through centuries long,
In Peace secure, in justice strong;
Around our gift of Freedom draw
The safeguards of Thy righteous law;
And, cast in some diviner mold,
Let the new cycle shame the old.

WELCOME TO THE NATION [1]

(Centennial Hymn sung on Independence Day, 1876.)

BY OLIVER WENDELL HOLMES

BRIGHT on the banners of lily and rose,
  Lo, the last sun of our country sets!
Wreathe the bright cannon that scowled on our foes,
  All but her friendships the Nation forgets,
  All but her friends, and their welcome, forgets.
These are around her: but where are her foes?
  Lo, while the sun of her century sets,
Peace, with her garlands of lily and rose!

Welcome! a shout like the war-trumpet's swell
  Wakes the wild echoes that slumber around!
Welcome! it quivers from Liberty's bell;
  Welcome! the walls of her temple resound!
  Hark! the gray walls of her temple resound!
Fade the far voices o'er hillside and dell;
  Welcome! still whisper the echoes around!
Welcome! still trembles on Liberty's bell!

Thrones of the continents! isles of the sea!
  Yours are the garlands of peace we entwine;
Welcome once more to the land of the free,
  Shadowed alike by the palm and the pine;
  Softly they murmur, the palm and the pine,
" Hushed is our strife, in the land of the free; "
  Over your children their branches entwine,
Thrones of the continents! isles of the sea!

[1] *By permission of the publishers, Houghton, Mifflin Co.*

LIBERTY'S LATEST DAUGHTER

BY BAYARD TAYLOR

(Third Canto.)

FORESEEN in the vision of sages,
  Foretold when martyrs bled,
She was born of the longing of ages,
  By the truth of the noble dead,
  And the faith of the living, fed!
No blood in her lightest veins
Frets at remembered chains,
Nor shame of bondage has bowed her head
  In her form and features still,
  The unblenching Puritan will,
Cavalier honor, Huguenot grace,
  The Quaker truth and sweetness,
And the strength of the danger-girdled race
  Of Holland, blend in a proud completeness.
From the homes of all, where her being began,
She took what she gave to man:
Justice that knew no station,
  Belief as soul decreed,
Free air for aspiration,
  Free force for independent deed.
She takes, but to give again,
As the sea returns the rivers in rain;
And gathered the chosen of her seed
From the hunted of every crown and creed.
Her Germany dwells by a gentler Rhine;
Her Ireland sees the old sunburst shine;
Her France pursues some dream divine;

Her Norway keeps his mountain-pine;
Her Italy waits by the western brine;
And, broad-based under all
　　Is planted England's oaken-hearted mood,
　　As rich in fortitude
As e'er went world-ward from the island wall.
　　Fused in her candid light,
　　To one strong race all races here united;
Tongues melt in hers; herditary foemen
　　Forget their sword and slogan, kith and clan;
'Twas glory, once, to be a Roman;
　　She makes it glory, now, to be a man.

———————

"SCUM O' THE EARTH"[1]

BY ROBERT HAVEN SCHAUFFLER

I

At the gate of the West I stand,
On the isle where the nations throng.
We call them "scum o' the earth";

Stay, are we doing you wrong,
Young fellow from Socrates' land?—
You, like a Hermes so lissome and strong
Fresh from the master Praxiteles' hand?
So you're of Spartan birth?
Descended, perhaps, from one of the band—

[1] *By permission of the publishers, Houghton, Mifflin Co.*

Deathless in story and song —
Who combed their long hair at Thermopylæ's
    pass? . . .
Ah, I forget the straits, alas!
More tragic than theirs, more compassion-worth,
That have doomed you to march in our "immigrant
    class"
Where you're nothing but "scum o' the earth."

II

You Pole with the child on your knee,
What dower bring you to the land of the free?
Hark! does she croon
That sad little tune
That Chopin once found on his Polish lea
And mounted in gold for you and for me?
Now a ragged young fiddler answers
In wild Czech melody
That Dvořak took whole from the dancers.
And the heavy faces bloom
In the wonderful Slavik way;
The little, dull eyes, the brows a-gloom,
Suddenly dawn like the day.
While, watching these folk and their mystery,
I forget that they're nothing worth;
That Bohemians, Slovaks, Croatians,
And men of all Slavik nations
Are "polacks"— and "scum o' the earth."

III

Genoese boy of the level brow,
Lad of the lustrous, dreamy eyes
Astare at Manhattan's pinnacles now
In the first, sweet shock of a hushed surprise;
Within your far-rapt seer's eyes
I catch the glow of the wild surmise
That played on the Santa Maria's prow
In that still gray dawn,
Four centuries gone,
When a world from the wave began to rise.
Oh, it's hard to foretell what high emprise
Is the goal that gleams
When Italy's dreams
Spread wing and sweep into the skies.
Cæsar dreamed him a world ruled well;
Dante dreamed Heaven out of Hell;
Angelo brought us there to dwell;
And you, are you of a different birth? —
You're only a " dago,"— and " scum o' the earth " !

IV

Stay, are we doing you wrong
Calling you " scum o' the earth,"
Man of the sorrow-bowed head,
Of the features tender yet strong,—
Man of the eyes full of wisdom and mystery
Mingled with patience and dread?
Have I not known you in history,
Sorrow-bowed head?
Were you the poet-king, worth
Treasures of Ophir unpriced?

Were you the prophet, perchance, whose art
Foretold how the rabble would mock
That shepherd of spirits, erelong,
Who should carry the lambs on his heart
And tenderly feed his flock?
Man — lift that sorrow-bowed head.
Lo! 'tis the face of the Christ!

The vision dies at its birth.
You're merely a butt for our mirth.
You're a " sheeny "— and therefore despised
And rejected as " scum o' the earth."

V

Countrymen, bend and invoke
Mercy for us blasphemers,
For that we spat on these marvelous folk,
Nations of darers and dreamers,
Scions of singers and seers,
Our peers, and more than our peers.
" Rabble and refuse," we name them
And " scum o' the earth," to shame them.
Mercy for us of the few, young years,
Of the culture so callow and crude,
Of the hands so grasping and rude,
The lips so ready for sneers
At the sons of our ancient more-than-peers.
Mercy for us who dare despise
Men in whose loins our Homer lies;
Mothers of men who shall bring to us
The glory of Titian, the grandeur of Huss;
Children in whose frail arms shall rest
Prophets and singers and saints of the West.

Newcomers all from the eastern seas,
Help us incarnate dreams like these.
Forget, and forgive, that we did you wrong.
Help us to father a nation, strong
In the comradeship of an equal birth,
In the wealth of the richest bloods of earth.

LIBERTY AND UNION ONE AND INSEPARABLE

BY DANIEL WEBSTER

I PROFESS, sir, in my career hitherto, to have kept steadily in view the prosperity and honor of the whole country, and the preservation of our Federal Union. It is to that Union that we owe our safety at home, and our consideration and dignity abroad. It is to that Union that we are chiefly indebted for whatever makes us most proud of our country. That Union we reached only by the discipline of our virtues, in the severe school of adversity. It had its origin in the necessities of disordered finance, prostrate commerce, and ruined credit. Under its benign influences these great interests immediately awoke, as from the dead, and sprang forth with newness of life. Every year of its duration has teemed with fresh proofs of its utility and its blessings; and, although our territory has stretched out wider and wider, and our population spread farther and farther, they have not outrun its protection or its benefits. It has been to us all a copious fountain of national, social, and personal happiness. I have not allowed myself, sir, to look beyond the Union, to see what might lie hidden in the dark recess behind. I have not coolly weighed the chances of preserving liberty, when the bonds that unite us together shall be broken asunder. I have not accustomed myself to hang over the precipice of disunion, to see whether, with my short sight, I can fathom the depth of the abyss below; nor could I regard him as a safe counselor in the affairs of this government, whose thought should be mainly bent on considering, not how the Union may be best preserved, but how tolerable might be the condition of the people when it should be broken up and destroyed.

While the Union lasts, we have high, exciting, gratifying prospects spread out before us, for us and our children. Beyond that I seek not to penetrate the veil. God grant that in my day, at least, that curtain may not rise! God grant that on my vision never may be opened what lies behind! When my eyes shall be turned to behold, for the last time, the sun in heaven, may I not see him shining on the broken and dishonored fragments of a once glorious Union; on States dissevered, discordant, belligerent; on a land rent with civil feuds, or drenched, it may be, in fraternal blood!

Let their last feeble and lingering glance rather behold the gorgeous ensign of the republic, now known and honored throughout the earth, still full high advanced, its arms and trophies streaming in their original luster, not a stripe erased or polluted, nor a single star obscured; bearing for its motto no such miserable interrogatory as, *What is all this worth?* nor those other words of delusion and folly,— *Liberty first and Union afterwards;* but everywhere, spread all over in characters of living light, blazing on all its ample folds as they float over the sea and over the land, and in every wind under the whole heavens, that other sentiment, dear to every true American heart,— *Liberty* and *Union, now* and *forever, one* and *inseparable!*

ADDRESS TO LIBERTY

BY WILLIAM COWPER

OH, could I worship aught beneath the skies
That earth hath seen, or fancy could devise,
Thine altar, sacred Liberty, should stand,
Built by no mercenary, vulgar hand,
With fragrant turf, and flowers as wild and fair
As ever dressed a bank, or scented summer air.

Duly, as ever on the mountain's height
The peep of morning shed a dawning light;
Again, when evening in her sober vest
Drew the gray curtain of the fading west;
My soul should yield thee willing thanks and praise
For the chief blessings of my fairest days:
But that were sacrilege: praise is not thine,
But His, who gave thee, and preserves thee mine;
Else I would say,— and, as I spake, bid fly
A captive bird into the boundless sky,—
This rising realm adores thee: thou art come
From Sparta hither, and art here at home;
We feel thy force still active; at this hour
Enjoys immunity from priestly power;
While conscience, happier than in ancient years,
Owns no superior but the God she fears.

Propitious Spirit! yet expunge a wrong
Thy rights have suffered, and our land, too long;
Teach mercy to ten thousand hearts, that share
The fears and hopes of a commercial care;
Prisons expect the wicked, and were built
To bind the lawless, and to punish guilt;
But shipwreck, earthquake, battle, fire, and flood
Are mighty mischiefs, not to be withstood:
And honest merit stands on slippery ground
Where covert guile and artifice abound.
Let just restraint, for public peace designed,
Chain up the wolves and tigers of mankind,—
The foe of virtue has no claim to thee,—
But let insolvent innocence go free.

THE TORCH OF LIBERTY

BY THOMAS MOORE

I saw it all in Fancy's glass —
    Herself, the fair, the wild magician,
Who bade this splendid day-dream pass,
    And named each gilded apparition.
'Twas like a torch-race,— such as they
    Of Greece performed, in ages gone,
When the fleet youths, in long array,
    Passed the bright torch triumphant on.

I saw the expectant nations stand
    To catch the coming flame in turn;
I saw, from ready hand to hand,
    The clear, though struggling, glory burn.

And oh, their joy, as it came near,
'Twas, in itself, a joy to see;
While Fancy whispered in my ear,
" That torch they pass is Liberty!"

And each, as she received the flame,
Lighted her altar with its ray;
Then, smiling, to the next who came,
Speeded it on its sparkling way.
From Albion first, whose ancient shrine
Was furnished with the flame already,
Columbia caught the boon divine,
And lit a flame, like Albion's, steady.

Shine, shine forever, glorious flame,
Divinest gift of gods to men!
From Greece thy earliest splendor came,
To Greece thy ray returns again.
Take, Freedom, take thy radiant round;
When dimmed, revive; when lost, return;
Till not a shrine through earth be found
On which thy glories shall not burn!

HOROLOGE OF LIBERTY

ANONYMOUS

THE world heard: the battle of Lexington — one;
the Declaration of Independence — two; the surrender
of Burgoyne — three; the siege of Yorktown — four;
the treaty of Paris — five; the inauguration of Washington — six; and then it was the sunrise of a new
day, of which we have seen yet only the glorious fore-
noon.

THE AMERICAN REPUBLIC

BY GEORGE BANCROFT

IN the fullness of time, a Republic rose up in the wilderness of America. Thousands of years had passed away before this child of the ages could be born. From whatever there was of good in the systems of former centuries she drew her nourishment; the wrecks of the past were her warnings. With the deepest sentiment of faith fixed in her inmost nature, she disenthralled religion from bondage to temporal power, that her worship might be worship only in spirit and in truth.

The wisdom which had passed from India through Greece, with what Greece had added of her own; the jurisprudence of Rome; the mediæval municipalities; the Teutonic method of representation, the political experience of England, the benignant wisdom of the expositors of the law of nature and of nations in France and Holland, all shed on her their selectest influence. She washed the gold of political wisdom from the sands wherever it was found; she cleft it from the rocks; she gleaned it among ruins. Out of all the discoveries of statesmen and sages, out of all the experience of past human life, she compiled a perennial political philosophy, the primordial principles of national ethics.

The wise men of Europe sought the best government in a mixture of monarchy, aristocracy, and democracy; and America went behind these names to extract from them the vital elements of social forms, and blend them harmoniously in the free Commonwealth, which comes nearest to the illustration of the natural equality of all men. She entrusted the guardianship of established rights to law; the movements of reform to the spirit of the people, and drew her force from the happy reconciliation of both.

A NEW NATIONAL HYMN

BY FRANCIS MARION CRAWFORD

HAIL, Freedom! thy bright crest
And gleaming shield, thrice blest,
   Mirror the glories of a world thine own.
Hail, heaven-born Peace! our sight,
Led by thy gentle light,
   Shows us the paths with deathless flowers strewn.
Peace, daughter of a strife sublime,
Abide with us till strife be lost in endless time.

Her one hand seals with gold
The portals of night's fold,
   Her other the broad gates of dawn unbars;
O'er silent wastes of snows,
Crowning her lofty brows,
   Gleams high her diadem of northern stars;
While, clothed in garlands of warm flowers,
Round Freedom's feet the South her wealth of beauty
    showers.

Sweet is the toil of peace,
Sweet is the year's increase,
   To loyal men who live by Freedom's laws;

And in war's fierce alarms
God gives stout hearts and arms
   To freemen sworn to save a rightful cause.
Fear none, trust God, maintain the right,
And triumph in unbroken Union's might.

Welded in war's fierce flame,
Forged on the hearth of fame,
   The sacred Constitution was ordained;
Tried in the fire of time,
Tempered in woes sublime,
   An age was passed and left it yet unstained.
God grant its glories still may shine,
While ages fade, forgotten, in time's slow decline!

Honor the few who shared
Freedom's first fight, and dared
   To face war's desperate tide at the full flood;
Who fell on hard-won ground,
And into Freedom's wound
   Poured the sweet balsam of their brave hearts' blood.
They fell; but o'er that glorious grave
Floats free the banner of the cause they died to save.

In radiance heavenly fair,
Floats on the peaceful air
   That flag that never stooped from Victory's pride;
Those stars that softly gleam,
Those stripes that o'er us stream,
   In war's grand agony were sanctified;
A holy standard, pure and free,
To light the home of peace, or blaze in victory.

Father, whose mighty power
Shields us through life's short hour,
   To Thee we pray: Bless us and keep us free;
All that is past forgive;
Teach us, henceforth, to live
   That, through our country, we may honor Thee;
And, when this mortal life shall cease,
Take Thou, at last, our souls to Thine eternal peace.

VII
FICTION

JIM'S AUNT

BY FRANCES BENT DILLINGHAM

"I WISH you could take him in," the minister said, almost entreatingly. "He isn't a bad boy, you know; his family is quite respectable; but when his aunt said she couldn't afford to take him into the country with her children, it seemed too bad for him to stay in the city."

"Oh, yes, of course," Miss Lucinda assented hastily. "If only he wasn't a boy!"

The minister sighed. "I want you to do what you think best."

It was Miss Lucinda's turn to sigh now — a long-drawn breath of surrender. "Well, I'll take him," she said.

The minister rose to go. "It's very kind of you, Miss Tarbox; be sure I appreciate your self-sacrifice;" and then he added, in a hesitating sort of way, "You are always full of good works."

The color flamed up in Miss Lucinda's face. "Oh!" she exclaimed, lifting her proud head still higher, "I don't do anything!" and the minister felt the usual sense of defeat he experienced in Miss Tarbox's presence.

He was quite dejected as he went down the garden walk. "So excellent a woman," he murmured to himself, and he mournfully contrasted her uncompromising manner with the flattering air of other single ladies of his parish as he glanced back furtively toward her parlor window.

But Miss Tarbox would have considered it unpardonable coquetry to peep after the minister, since he was an unmarried man, and she an eligible if not youthful spinster, so she went at once into the kitchen to prepare her supper. But the color did not at once fade from her cheeks as she moved about in her rapid, methodical manner, and she thought not so much of the boy who was to come, as of the man who had just gone. If the minister felt overcome in Miss Lucinda's presence, she, too, had a similar feeling after he had left her with some unspoken word on his lips.

"It seems as though he was going to say something sometimes, but I kill it out of him. I wonder what is the matter with me, anyway?" Miss Lucinda had acquired a habit of talking to herself, and now nodded gravely to her reflection in the little mirror over the kitchen shelf. "I'm not bad-looking and I mean to be pleasant, but, somehow most folks seem kind of afraid of me. I s'pose I have an up-and-coming way with me that scares most of them. I don't seem to be the sort they take to; though I must say it's forlorn to be that way," and the image in the mirror sighed audibly.

When Miss Lucinda had seated herself at her lonely tea-table, her thoughts took another channel. "What in the world am I to do with a boy? He'll upset things on the table-cloth, and let flies in the house and rub his fingers on the window-pane, and holler. Well, there's one thing about it, he's got to mind every word I say to him!" But here Miss Lucinda drew herself up with a jerk. "There you go, Lucinda, complaining of your loneliness, and then finding fault when someone comes to see you; thinking you're too fond of running things, and then saying you're going to make this boy do just as you want him to."

It was only a few days later when the boy came, in company with the minister. He was not so large a boy as Miss Lucinda had expected from his age, and he was rather thin and pale.

" I'll give him enough to eat, that's one thing," she told the minister. " And I've been thinking there's one comfort in a boy: he doesn't talk so much as a girl — that is, he isn't likely to."

" No, he isn't likely to," the minister assented, a little doubtfully.

After the minister had gone, Miss Lucinda began to wonder what she should do with the boy the rest of the morning. She found him in the kitchen, his short legs stretched to their utmost, trying to capture two flies buzzing on the window-pane. He paused in his exertions, and turned on her with a beaming smile.

" Hullo! Is dinner ready?" he asked.

Miss Lucinda drew herself up. " We don't have dinner till twelve o'clock," she said frigidly.

" Oh, that's all right; you needn't hurry," the boy said pleasantly. " I'm kinder grub-struck, but I guess I kin wait."

Miss Lucinda stared at him in rebuke. " Perhaps you'd better go out and play," she suggested, " while I get dinner; " and off he went.

When the dinner-table was laid, Miss Lucinda rang her seldom-used bell out of the back door, and the boy came in promptly, with quite a color in his cheeks.

" My! " he exclaimed, staring at the neat, plentiful table, " ain't this a feed! "

" You'd better go and wash your hands," Miss

Lucinda suggested, and the boy went cheerily to the sink, scrubbing himself vigorously and then wiping his hands on the spick-and-span roller. Miss Lucinda groaned at the great black marks on the towel, and went out into the kitchen to turn it about so that she might not have to look at them through the dining-room doorway.

"Mercy on us!" she cried in distress as she came out into the kitchen, "you've left the door open. The house'll be full of flies!"

"Now, don't you trouble," the boy said soothingly. "I'll catch every single fly that's got in. I'm a great flycatcher, I am. I'm used to flies."

At the table, conversation did not at all flourish. Miss Lucinda had heard of a boy's appetite, but she had never dreamed of such awful capacity as this young person displayed. After he had taken the first keen edge from his hunger he laid down his knife and fork and looked at her inquiringly.

"Should you mind if I was to call you aunt?" he asked smilingly. "You know I useter live with my aunt, and I'm kinder useter sayin' it."

"I think it would be better if you called me Miss Tarbox," Miss Lucinda said, surprised, but not thrown off her guard.

"That's rather long," the boy said meditatively; "but I guess if I say it often enough I kin git it Miss Tarbox, Misstarbox, Misstubox, Misstibox, Miss —"

"Don't say that over again, for goodness' sake," Miss Lucinda said irritably. "What is your name?"

"Well, the whole of it is James Wilson, but I guess you'd better call me Jim. I'm useter that."

"What did you do this morning?" Miss Tarbox

felt called upon to sustain and direct further conversation.

"I went over to see the boy 'cross the street and we're goin' to play Indian this afternoon. Did you ever play Indian?"

Miss Tarbox shook her head.

"You stick feathers all 'round your hat, and you make a fire and roast potatoes, and yell and eat the potatoes. That boy is a mighty nice feller. I told him I was stoppin' with you and goin' to have a dandy time. I guess he don't know you very well. I told him I thought you was kinder hard to git acquainted with. He said we'd git our feathers out o' his henyard, and I thought p'r'aps I might bring the potatoes. Do you think you could let me have two potatoes? I won't eat quite so much next time."

Miss Lucinda drew a long breath. "Yes," she said, "I'll let you have the potatoes."

"Now that's real nice. I told him I thought you'd be willin'."

As soon as dinner was over Miss Lucinda brought the two potatoes from the cellar, but the boy did not go at once; he sat on a chair in the kitchen, and watched her brisk movements as she cleared the table and made ready to wash the dishes.

"Say, you're awful smart, ain't you?" he asked after a moment of observation, and Miss Tarbox, somewhat overwhelmed did not reply.

He placed his elbow on his round knee and his chin on his small hand and stared a few moments in silence.

"It looks awful kinder nice the way you hold up your head. Now, my aunt, she kinder slumps along.

She's a real nice woman, you know, but she don't look's though she had much gumption."

Another silence.

"Say, what kin I do?" he asked next.

"Mercy on us!" ejaculated Miss Lucinda, "don't ask me. I thought you were going to roast potatoes."

"I thought p'r'aps you might be kinder lonesome all alone, and I'd jest as soon help you wash up. I'm useter it. I kin make beds and sweep and wash dishes and do lots o' things. Try me and see."

"Thank you, I can get along very well; you needn't help," Miss Lucinda said in grim accents of dismissal but the boy did not move.

"I s'pose you're pretty busy," he ventured presently.

"Well, yes, rather," Miss Lucinda answered shortly.

"Do you usually have a real good time Fourth o' July?" he went on.

Miss Lucinda gasped. "Well, no. I can't say I do," she answered in mournful truthfulness.

"Now that's funny," the boy said, in a surprised tone. "Seem's though the country'd be an awful nice place to have a good time in, Fourth o' July. Mebbe it's 'cause you never had nobody to cel'brate with; but you will this year. You'll have a real nice time, too; I always enjoy Fourth o' July."

Miss Lucinda gave a feeble sigh. "What do you usually do Fourth o' July?" she asked, with the desire to learn her coming fate.

"Well, last year I had one bunch o' firecrackers that got fired off the very first thing. I thought mebbe this year I'd earn 'nough money to buy two bunches; d'you think I could?"

"Well, really, I don't know," Miss Lucinda said.

"And last year I went to see the percession, and the

crowd jammed me, and I didn't see nothin'; but this year they're goin' to have a percession out here, and that feller asked me to be in it. D'you suppose I could?"

" I don't know," Miss Lucinda answered again.

" They're goin' to have reg'lar uniforms, red, white, and blue "— evidently the boy took this as half consent —" and it's goin' to be jest great. I s'pose it'd be a good deal o' trouble to make me a uniform, seein's you're so busy?"

" A soldier suit? Dear me, yes, I should say so!" There was no doubt now in Miss Lucinda's tones.

The boy drew a deep breath as he rose to go. " All right," he said cheerfully, " I'll tell the fellers; p'r'aps they'll let me march, jest the same."

When supper-time came and Miss Lucinda rang her bell again out the door, she saw the boy coming along the path from the barn, helping Joshua, the man-of-all-work, bring in the brimming pail of milk.

" Supper is ready," Miss Lucinda said, and this time the boy washed his hands without special order.

" Say," he cried, waving the roller, " Josh's goin' to teach me how to milk, and you won't have to hire him any more. I kin do everything's well as not, can't I, Josh?" But Joshua had, fortunately, gone and did not hear this threat to usurp his position.

" Well, you do have orful good meals," he said, sitting down opposite Miss Lucinda's handsome, severe figure. " I'm orful hungry, but I did have the dandiest time to-day you ever heard of. The potatoes didn't roast very well, but the fire burned like fun. My Jiminy —"

" James!" called Miss Lucinda in an awful voice.

James opened his innocent eyes and looked at her,

then fell to eating with renewed vigor, and it was some time before he mustered courage to finish his recital.

But when he came out into the kitchen and watched her moving back and forth in the dusky light, Miss Lucinda somehow felt herself moved to open conversation.

"You didn't eat so very much for supper, James."

"No, marm," James answered promptly. "Don't you remember them potatoes? I was a-payin' for 'em."

"Mercy on us!" cried Miss Lucinda, and she went to the dining-room and brought from the table the currant pie, of which the boy, to Miss Lucinda's amazement, had eaten only two pieces.

He ate the third generous slice she gave him, and again sat still, watching her with round, admiring eyes as she moved about.

"I think it's about time for you to go to bed now, James," his guardian said presently, and James rose promptly.

"Would you mind calling me Jim? It sounds kinder homesick to be called James," he said, with sudden wistfulness engendered, even in his boyish spirit, by the shadows and the newness of the place.

"Good-night, Jim," Miss Lucinda responded; but Jim still stood looking at her with serious eyes.

"My aunt useter kiss me good-night. You don't exactly look like the kissin' kind, and I ain't neither, but — but I didn't know, seein' 's you're so good to me, but — p'r'aps " — he flushed and shifted himself from one foot to the other.

Miss Lucinda flushed, too, and looked greatly embarrassed, but hers was no stony heart to refuse so gallant a suitor; she stooped and kissed him awkwardly and flutteringly somewhere upon his forehead or hair; but when she would have felt her duty over, he suddenly seized her in an impetuous hug. He went upstairs quickly, and Miss Lucinda sat down in her little rocking-chair with hot, red cheeks, and something deeper than embarrassment brought a new light into her clear eyes.

"I think he tries hard to be a good boy," Miss Lucinda said to the minister when he next called, " but he does a great many things that are rather startling, and now and then he says something he oughtn't to."

"Yes?" the minister said, in kindly interest.

"The very first day he got here, he swore at the table." The minister looked horrified. "Of course I spoke of it right off and he hasn't done it again. He was kind of excited about playing Indian, and I don't suppose he really meant it; he said "— the minister reddened and looked away, and Miss Lucinda flushed —"he said ' Jiminy.' " The minister drew out his handkerchief and coughed slightly. "But, as I say, he hasn't said anything since, and I think I could get along very well if Fourth of July wasn't coming so soon. But what do you think? He wants a soldier suit, and firecrackers, and all sorts of things. If only he hadn't come till after the Fourth! I never did approve of it. I always did think it was a heathenish holiday," and Miss Lucinda broke off feelingly.

After the minister had gone Miss Lucinda started to go to the village store. Jim usually did the errands, but this was something that had been overlooked, and he was at play, out of calling distance.

On Miss Lucinda's return, as she came through the lane by a shorter road, she heard voices in the field beyond; the speakers were hidden by a hedge, but she recognized the tones as Jim's and his playfellow's across the street.

" Say, can't you march ? " said a wheedling voice.

" No, I guess not," Jim's voice answered, a trifle dolefully.

" Why not? Won't she make you a suit ? "

There was a little pause before Jim answered: " Well, I don't know's I care 'bout marchin'."

" H'm! you needn't say that. It's cause that stingy old maid won't make you anything to wear, I know."

There was a sudden movement on the other side of the hedge. " You call her a stingy old maid again and you'll 'see! She's a handsome lady, she is, and it ain't none o' your business if I don't want to march."

" H'm! you needn't git on your ear so dreadful quick. I wouldn't stand up for anybody that only let me earn money enough to buy two bunches of fire-crackers. Why, I've got two packages! A great Fourth o' July you'll have! "

" I've got some more money, but I ain't goin' to buy firecrackers; I'm savin' it for a s'prise. Say, look-a-here, you see, Miss Tibbox ain't never had a boy 'round, an' she don't understand 'bout Fourth o' July, that's all."

Miss Lucinda did not wait to hear the answer, but went swiftly back to the village.

The night before the Fourth, as Jim was going to bed, Miss Lucinda said: " Ain't you going to march with the boys to-morrow, Jim? "

Jim shook his head and looked at her solemnly. " I ain't got no suit. The fellers won't let you march without one. Never mind, I've given up lots of things. My aunt wa'nt much of a hand for doin' things, you know."

Jim had never asked Miss Lucinda to kiss him good-night since that first time, when he felt so markedly homesick, and certainly she would never have offered to kiss him, so she merely said, as he took his light to go upstairs, " Good-night, Jim."

But she sat down in her rocking-chair, quite near the dining-room door, with an expectant listening expression on her face. Suddenly there arose a great commotion above, and Jim came tumbling down the stairs with wild shrieks of delight.

" Oh, my gracious! oh, my gracious!" he cried. "Look-a-here, did you do it? Ain't they butes? I kin march now, can't I? Oh, my Jimi — my gracious, my gracious!" And he danced about the room, first on one foot and then on the other, waving in one hand a wonderful pair of red, white, and blue trousers, in the other a similarly gorgeous jacket.

Miss Lucinda was really frightened; she was not used to such demonstrations of joy. But Jim stopped his dancing presently, and, throwing his cherished outfit on the floor, he embraced her rapturously, until she gravely extricated herself.

" I'm glad you like it, Jim," she said a little stiffly.

" Like it!" Jim shrieked, throwing himself about in another wild pantomime. " Like it! Oh, my gracious, I'm 'fraid I shall bust!"

" I think you had better go to bed now," Miss Lucinda said, after a pause.

Jim gathered up his suit and looked at her anxiously. " Should you mind if I was to git up dreadful early, if I didn't wake you up?" he asked.

And Miss Lucinda, to her own amazement, found

herself replying: "Well, no; but don't get up too early."

And after Jim was asleep, and it was time for her to retire, she went softly into his room to lay two packages of firecrackers on the chair beside the gay garments.

Poor Miss Lucinda hid her head under the bedclothes during the night, and when there came an extra loud explosion thought of Jim. But at breakfast-time he turned up safe and smiling.

"I never had sech a good time in all my life before. Say, Miss Tibbox, did you mean all those firecrackers for me? Well, if you ain't the nicest woman in the world! I've got a s'prise for you, too. Just you wait and see!" and he nodded mysteriously across the table at Miss Lucinda, who felt a vague misgiving.

"Why didn't you wear your soldier suit?" she asked.

Jim beamed upon her. "Why, I'm a-savin' it. We don't march till ten o'clock. You don't know how much nicer it is to be in a percession than jest to look at it. I wish you could march, too," he added politely. "But you'll come out on the piazza and watch us go by, won't you?"

And Miss Lucinda promised to be on the spot.

If Jim had never passed another such day, it was as wholly unprecedented in Miss Lucinda Tarbox's calendar. Jim marched by the house as proud as a peacock in his new soldier suit, and raised a cheer to Miss Lucinda so loud and hearty that she retired blushing into the house. Then after dinner there was nothing for Miss Lucinda but to come out on the piazza and watch Jim fire off some of his crackers;

and there the poor lady sat cringing and shrinking and trying to smile each time Jim would shout, " That's the loudest of all ! "

But the climax of the day was reached when Jim brought the minister home to supper. How it happened that the minister appeared upon the scene at tea-time, Miss Lucinda could not understand ; but when he arrived, and Jim whispered in a loud aside, " I thought p'r'aps he might stay to supper," there was no alternative but a cordial invitation, which the minister accepted promptly. Miss Lucinda likewise never knew the remarks with which Jim escorted the minister to the house. " She's the very nicest woman in the world," he told the minister, " and I think she thinks you're a pretty nice sort of a chap." The minister never repeated these compliments of Jim's to Miss Lucinda.

After tea, Jim's secret was revealed; he had invested the larger part of his small earnings in fireworks, which he was quite sure Miss Lucinda would enjoy, and he had invited the minister to supper that he might help him set them off. So Miss Lucinda came out on the porch in the darkness, and the minister and Jim paraded about in the neat little garden in front, and proceeded to diminish Jim's purchases. Presently the minister came up on the piazza and sat down beside Miss Lucinda, for the remaining fireworks could easily be disposed of by Jim. But just as the minister was considering whether the time was propitious for an advancement of his own interests, there came a sudden sharp cry from Miss Lucinda, and he turned to see a line of flame running about the paper belt of the gallant little showman. The minister was quick in his movements, and was down

the path and had Jim in his arms and the fire
smothered in a few moments, while Miss Lucinda was
by his side, sobbing and bending over Jim's little
form.

"Oh, let me see him," she cried; "the dear child!
Is he hurt very badly?"

Jim wriggled a little in the minister's arms, and
opening his eyes, smiled on her. "Now don't you
worry," he said cheerily, "I ain't hurt."

"But I'm 'fraid I've spoilt my suit," he added when
the minister had placed him on the lounge in Miss
Lucinda's little sitting-room.

"Oh, never mind the suit!" Miss Lucinda cried, and
Jim looked up at her in reproachful surprise.

But it was quite true that he was not hurt, though
rather weak from the fright, and presently he came
out again, between the minister and Miss Lucinda, to
sit on the piazza and watch the neighbors' fireworks.

Jim, on the little stool at Miss Lucinda's feet, leaned
his head against her knee. "I don't care, it's been a
fine Fourth o' July," he murmured.

"So it has," echoed the minister; "don't you think
so, Lucinda?" But Miss Lucinda's only answer was
a blush and a consenting silence.

"Do you mind now if I call you aunt?" Jim's voice
asked.

Miss Lucinda laid her hand gently on Jim's head.
"No, dear," she said softly; "no."

"You might call me uncle," suggested the minister.

Jim nodded brightly. "All right," he said promptly;
"then we'll be a reg'lar family."

And the new uncle and aunt smiled in the darkness.

VIII
THE NEW FOURTH

OUR BARBAROUS FOURTH

BY MRS. ISAAC L. RICE

(From *The Century Magazine,* June, 1908.)

In his first book, Marcus Aurelius gratefully acknowledges his obligation to Sextus of Chæronea for having taught him to "express approbation without noisy display." Alas! in all the centuries which have elapsed since the time of this emperor-philosopher, we have not yet learned to appreciate the wisdom of his counsel; and every holiday, in our country, at least, is made the occasion of a strident outburst of hoodlumism. Hallowe'en, Election Day, Christmas, New Year's, Inauguration Day, and Fourth of July, each witnesses our thoroughfares thronged with shouting and disorderly crowds, provided with every noisy device from the tin trumpet to the dangerous pistol, while shrieks of whistles shrill maddeningly above the street clamor and the booming of bells. Accidents occur, the sick are made worse by these frenzied demonstrations, and the young fail to appreciate the significance of the day which is being so unbeautifully celebrated.

Of all these "noise-fests," the most shocking is the Fourth of July, and its grim statistics probably furnish a sadder commentary on human folly than that afforded by any other celebration in the world.

I often wonder what would be the emotions of a stranger, quite ignorant of our institutions, if he arrived in our country — "God's Country," as we affectionately call it — just before midsummer, and glanced over our great newspapers. After reading some items, such as the following, would he be apt to await a great and glorious anniversary, or the advent of a day of strife and terror?

The horrible Fourth will soon be here. . . . In all the big cities the Fourth of July is now looked forward to with apprehension and looked back upon with a shudder, and even with horror.

Or,

The Board of Health has established supply stations of tetanus antitoxin throughout the city. The National Volunteer Emergency Service has established field dressing stations in the thickly populated sections. The hospitals also expect their usual busy day.

And then he would read head-lines like these:

THE NATIONAL BATTLE-FIELD
CARNAGE BEGINS ON HOLIDAY EVE.
BLOODIEST FOURTH YET
DEATHS AND INJURIES IN FOURTH OF
JULY'S WAKE

After our stranger had grasped the fact that this was not the record of a battle or other public calamity, but merely some details regarding the manner in which a great nation commemorates the most solemn event in its history, I doubt whether he would have an exalted opinion of a people who could desecrate so noble a memory by so barbarous an observance.

The fitting celebration of Independence Day is a question on which patriotic Americans are separated into two widely divergent parties, one claiming that it ought to be observed as noisily as possible, the other believing that our national birthday is too glorious an occasion to be marred by din and disorder. Of course we know that even among those who favor a boisterous observance there are many who cannot tolerate it themselves, and escape to the country in order to avoid the tortures of the "awful Fourth"; just as we know that a large proportion of the noise-makers, including the small boy and the big boy, too, is heedless, if not ignorant, of all that our holiday stands for, and thinks of it only as a time when clamor may reign unrestrained.[1]

The figures which indicate the price that we pay for each of our yearly celebrations are so appalling that one would suppose a knowledge of them would be the most powerful deterrent to our annual massacre. This, unfortunately, is not the case. For the past five pears, the *Journal of the American Medical Association* has endeavored to collect statistics setting forth what the celebration of the Fourth costs in life and human usefulness; and although these are admittedly incomplete,— compiled, as they are, almost entirely from newspaper reports instead of from

[1] *The following is an instance of this: Last Fourth of July, a police court magistrate, wishing to know how many of the prisoners before him, charged with shooting in the streets, could possibly plead patriotic motives, asked each in turn to state his nationality. Of the twenty in line, only two were American-born.*

records of hospitals, dispensaries, and physicians,—they form the gravest possible arraignment of the recklessness which is willing to pay such a price for a "jolly day." They show that during the celebration of five national birthdays, from 1903 to 1907 inclusive, eleven hundred and fifty-three persons were killed, and twenty-one thousand five hundred and twenty were injured! Of the injured, eighty-eight suffered total, and three hundred and eighty-nine partial, blindness; three hundred and eight persons lost arms, legs, or hands, and one thousand and sixty-seven lost one or more fingers. But these figures, startling as they are, convey only a faint idea of the suffering, both physical and mental, which went to swell the total cost of these five holidays; in this we must also include the weeks and often months of anguish of the injured, the suspense of entire families while the fate of some loved one hung in the balance, the horror of a future of sightless years, the pinching poverty now the lot of many because of the death or maiming of the breadwinner.

But putting aside the question of fatalities, of invalidism, of blindness, of penury, the effect on the sick of a long continuance of explosive noises, varying in intensity for days, or even weeks, and deafening for twenty-four hours at least, merits serious consideration. That the return of our "glorious Fourth" is looked forward to with dread by our hospital-sick, as well as by those who are concerned in their care, was made pathetically clear to me last summer when I interviewed the superintendents of almost all our municipal institutions. One and all deplored the needless suffering inflicted on their patients by our barbarous manner of celebration, and begged me to bring the matter to the attention of the Police Department.[1]

In this connection, a letter from Dr. Thomas Darlington, Commissioner of Health, is of interest:

> I agree entirely with you in regard to the serious injury inflicted upon patients in the hospitals occasioned by the common practice of exploding firecrackers and torpedoes in the immediate vicinity.

Professor William Hanna Thomson took the same stand when he stated:

> I rejoice to hear that your Society for the Suppression of Unnecessary Noise proposes to have measures taken to lessen the explosions of firecrackers and firearms in the neighborhood of our city hospitals on the Fourth of July. Such noises are particularly injurious, both from their nature and their being of an unusual kind, to patients with any high fever, such as typhoid, and it will be a great service to humanity to have them suppressed, if not altogether, as most sane people will acknowledge, yet at least near institutions harboring a variety of patients.

One feature of our celebration which has not yet been touched upon is the cost. Last year, New York

---

[1] *I may here say, in passing, that our Police Commissioner, recognizing the humane necessity of properly safeguarding the sick, sent out officers with orders to prevent disturbances in the vicinity of hospitals. Thanks to his action, the city's sick had a day of comparative peace, and the reports which I received that night were unanimous in stating that the hospitals had never had such a quiet Fourth. A letter written by Mother Celso, Mother-Superior of St. Elizabeth's Hospital, will show how gratefully General Bingham's thoughtfulness was appreciated:* "It seems as if we were in Paradise. The patients, the doctors, and the sisters all appreciate the quietness of the day."

City boasted of an outlay of four million dollars, while the country as a whole burned up the huge sum of twenty million dollars in fireworks. Finally, we must add the vast sum lost by conflagrations before we are in a position to realize the whole price that we pay for our day of jollity.

It is interesting to remark how strongly the press is beginning to voice its protest against our "noise-fest"— a protest now largely seconded by public opinion, although a few years ago it would have been regarded as woefully unpatriotic. Here are a few excerpts gathered last July from widely scattered papers, which are unanimous in decrying our present-day observance:

The most ridiculous and senseless celebration of any great national event.— *New York Commercial*.

What the connection is between explosives and patriotism, no one has ever undertaken to describe.— *Utica Press*.

The people must be educated to appreciate the folly of dynamite as a factor in patriotism.— *Chicago Daily Tribune*.

Time to consider how our annual worship of the God of Noise is to be abolished. This blatant and death-dealing Divinity long ago usurped the shrine occupied by Patriotism. Every year we carry and lay on his bloody altars human sacrifices, like the tribute of maidens to the Minotaur — only they are mostly boys. And so, year after year, the "Glorious Fourth" becomes more and more a dread festival of blood and fire and noise, of death and mayhem.— *Minneapolis Journal*.

The traditional gunpowder and dynamite orgies of Independence Day are wrong. Firearms and explosives have no place in any sane scheme of city life.— *Cleveland Plain Dealer*.

The day on which human folly too frequently runs amuck. . . . That the achievement of our national independence, brought about through the necessary spilling of great quantities of blood, should be commemorated by the very general loss of life and limb is as unnecessary as it is deplorable.— *Union* (Manchester, N. H.).

Americans are realizing that noises, maimed and wounded children, and big conflagrations should not be the sequence of the Nation's birthday.— *Toledo Blade*.

What ought to be the most enjoyable day in the calendar, is made a day of general carnage and a day toward which adults look forward with dread and whose passing they look back upon with a sense of mighty relief.— *Pioneer Press* (St. Paul, Minn.).

It is the money burned up in useless and dangerous explosives that is wasted, serving no better purpose than to leave the city with a headache the morning after.— *Republic* (St. Louis).

The din . . . is hideously vulgar and utterly uncivilized . . . discreditable to those who make it and to the civil authorities who permit it.— *Evening Wisconsin* (Milwaukee).

I fain would haul down the red flag of our modern Fourth of July and, in its place, run up the flag of peace, quietude, rest, contentment, and personal safety.— *Life* (New York).

The total results of our last "jolly celebration" of Independence Day were 164 killed and 4,249 injured, many of them being maimed for life! Is this method of celebration really worth while? — *Journal Amer. Med. Assn.* (Chicago).

How can any satisfaction be taken in the perversion of a holiday to purposes of disorder and destruction, and how can any pride be felt in methods of observance which inevitably condemn hundreds — if not thousands — to be shot, burned, maimed, and otherwise disfigured and tor-

tured in propitiation of the great god of senseless uproar?
— *New York Tribune.*

As for those who are in favor of continuing our
present mode of celebration, I can find but one who
has written openly in its defense, and even then there
is a suspicion that the article is ironical.

It is better to shock the sensitive nerves of a few grown
people than to have the boys and girls grow up molly-
coddles, with the fear of gunpowder in their hearts and
no appreciation of a boisterous holiday, rich in patriotic
appeal, and full of the " rough house " spirit of healthy
Americanism.

This, if seriously meant, reaches the height of
absurdity; for if there is one thing of which little children should have a wholesome dread, it is gunpowder,
and I know of no other country in which such a
weapon is put into the hands of babes.

It is customary with us to excuse ourselves for
Fourth of July accidents by putting all the blame on
the small boy. This, however, seems scarcely fair.
The blame for much of the annual massacre rests not
upon the careless small boy, but upon the careless
big parent who places in his hand the instrument of
destruction. And an even greater share of the blame
is due to public apathy, which not only allows the
annual suspension of sane and safe ordinances regu-
lating the use of firearms and explosives, but also permits the disorderly few to injure the health and
disturb the repose of the orderly many.

As proving that noise is the great desideratum in
fireworks, a few extracts from various catalogues will

prove interesting. Here, for instance, is a piece the figures of which, according to the thrilling description, move about "whistling and screaming in fantastic, wild, unearthly furore, terminating with a fusillading report," and another which bursts "with terrific reports that can be heard for miles," while a third explodes "with reports equal to six- and twelve-pound cannons," and a fourth like "an imitation rapid-fire Gatling-gun." An appreciative testimonial lauds a "Salute of LYDDITE SHELLS, nothing giving such a tremendous report having ever before been heard in our celebration," while other goods are emphatically praised as being "loudest and best," or "big in noise." One particular piece is noticeable because it consists of a string of fifty thousand firecrackers. As corroborative of all this, which tends to show that noise is what is desired above all else in fireworks, comes this published interview with a dealer, which is certainly illuminating:

The exploding cane is always a winner so long as it is not suppressed by the police. Blank cartridges come up at the head of the list. Nothing gives a celebrator so much pleasure as flourishing a pistol and shooting several times in rapid succession. There is just one thing that determines the efficiency of any contrivance designed for celebrating the Fourth, and that is, the volume of sound it makes. For that reason the cannon firecrackers are popular, and always will remain so.

This, then, is what excites the patriotic fervor of the partisans of a strident Fourth, though it does seem as if their enthusiasm would be somewhat lessened in

placing side by side with the above this extract from
the *Journal of the American Medical Association,*
which considers the causative factors of the aftermath of last Independence Day:

Of the 102 deaths aside from tetanus, gunshot wounds
caused twenty, giant crackers caused thirteen, and thirteen deaths were due to explosions of powder, torpedoes
and dynamite. Ten deaths were due to falls or runaways
caused by firecrackers. . . . The limit of tolerance
is reached, however, when we know that thirty-one persons were burned to death. . . . The principal cause
of the most mutilating wounds is by far the giant cracker.
. . . This year 1,489 injuries, including thirteen deaths
and eight cases of lockjaw, were due to the giant cracker.

It is a reflection scarcely calculated to gratify our
national pride that the United States is the only civilized country which observes the greatest of its fête-
days in such an uncivilized fashion. Our sister republics, France, Switzerland, and Brazil, rejoice full
as heartily as we over their national birthdays, but
they celebrate them in a sane, safe, wholesome, and
happy way, and not in our barbarous manner. As regards the observance of the French fête, July 14th,
Marcel Prévost, the eminent writer, has kindly described it for me in the following letter:

The fête of July 14th is, above all, in France, a day of
popular rejoicing; politics do not enter into it. It affords
an opportunity of illuminating the town-halls and public
buildings, and of indulging in the pleasure of dancing in
the open air. In a word, it is a huge kermess. It has
always taken place in order and tranquillity. Accidents
are rare, even in Paris. And since the review at Long-

champs has humanely been arranged to take place at nine in the morning, instead of at noon, the troops do not run the risk of sunstroke, which sometimes saddened the early fêtes of July 14th.

The following touchingly beautiful account of the observance of Switzerland's birthday was sent me by Dr. Eugène Richard, Member of the Council of State:

Year by year the people of Switzerland keep the anniversary of 1291, which was in real truth the foundation of the Confederation. Does that treaty — founded by the inhabitants of the Forest Cantons, borrowing from justice her most equitable principles (even down to that of arbitration between states), and guaranteed by the rigid energy of its signers — receive a commemoration worthy of its splendid simplicity?

No clamorous ceremony, to drown the voices of the past, instead of blending with them. We give proof of our remembrance of the First of August by a few brief manifestations during the closing hours of the day.

This national solemnity, surprising as it may seem, finds no place in the list of legal holidays. No one interrupts his daily tasks, for such was the way with the men of 1291, who, returning to their homes, took up again the care of their herds.

As night descends, the bells on all the churches are set to pealing in a sublime concert of gratitude, rising with penetrating poetry through the serenity and softness of a summer night. Shortly afterward bonfires are kindled along the heights. Here and there will be a modest illumination or rare display of fireworks. Occasionally an orator reminds the people of the significance of their rejoicing and holds up for imitation the character of our ancestors.

Whoever witnesses this spectacle realizes the strength and the sincerity of a patriotism that, without clamor or ostentation, draws fresh life by reverting to its original sources. Switzerland lives in the heart of her citizens. A noisy demonstration would take from us the benefit of a thoughtful mood.

In order to produce an impression both profound and salutary, national celebrations must needs have a pervading tranquillity, which enhances their dignity, and leads mankind to earnest thought.

According to a very charming letter from his Excellency, Señor Joaquin Nabuco, Brazilian Ambassador, it appears that although his countrymen do not observe their festivals with that calm, patriotic fervor which characterizes the Swiss, and although they rejoice in noise as well as in color, there is nothing to show that their holidays are marred by that disorder and by those horrible lists of casualties and accidents which disgrace the celebration of our great anniversary.

The following delightful description of Germany's greatest festival, the Emperor's birthday, has been given me by Professor Hugo Münsterberg of Harvard University:

When I look backward to my boyhood days in Germany and ask myself from what sources my young patriotism was steadily supplied, I cannot value highly enough the influence of the patriotic celebrations in my school and my native town. The dearest memory belongs to the Emperor's birthday. I know quite well that the present Emperor was born in January; but when I hear the word "Emperor's birthday," it still always awakes in me first the date of the 22d of March — the old Emperor's day.

Long before, the school planned everything for the grand day; patriotic and religious music, songs and pa-

triotic declamations by the younger pupils, short dramatic
plays with motives from German history, given by the
older boys, and always an enthusiastic oration by one of
the teachers. In Sunday clothes we gathered in the
school; everything was decorated with flowers and garlands and flags, and the whole school continuously, year
by year, was lifted up in a common pride and enthusiasm.
Two or three of the happiest morning hours were devoted
to the celebration, and the jubilant hurrah for the beloved
Emperor at the end of the historic oration was the only
sound of the day.

Then we streamed out into the decorated streets, enjoyed the picturesque parades and went to the concert at
the market-place, where patriotic marches kindled our
youthful emotions. The afternoon belonged to parties at
home, where school friends gathered and enjoyed their
games with a historic flavor and the chocolate with a patriotic abundance of cakes. Quiet, mellow days they were,
and any loud noise would have appeared to us boys as
a desecration of the festivity; and yet the loyalty which
I stored up in those March days of my boyhood still sup-
plies me amply when I have, year for year on the 27th
of January, to make my Emperor's birthday orations to
the German-Americans.

An interesting account of the manner in which
Japan celebrates her fêtes was kindly written for me
by his Excellency Viscount Aoki, recently Japanese
Ambassador to the United States:

In Japan we have three great national holidays. They
are November 3d, the present Emperor's birthday; New
Year's Day; and February 11th, the Day of the Accession
of the Emperor Jimmu, the first ruler of the Empire of
Japan.

An illustration of the Emperor's birthday celebration

in Japan will be sufficient to give a general idea as to how our national holidays are celebrated at home, for there is little difference in the way of its celebration between the above-named three holidays, except in minor details:

On the Emperor's birthday all offices, schools, banks, and large business houses are closed. The national flag is hoisted on all public buildings, schools, and on most of the private houses all over the country. High dignitaries, both civil and military, who are present in the capital, proceed to the Palace of Tokio to present before the throne their congratulations for the occasion, while those in the country and abroad send their congratulatory messages by mail through the Minister for the Imperial Household. In every school all over the country the day is observed in a form appropriate to the occasion. One hundred and one salutes are fired from every fort in the empire. The imperial review of the army is in regular order of the celebration of the day, when hundreds of thousands of the enthusiastic public gather around the drill-ground and all along the imperial route to cheer their august and beloved sovereign and to witness the glorious military parade of the day, while all of his Majesty's ships fire twenty-one salutes (otherwise known as the national salute) and appear in full dress. The Emperor entertains in the palace at breakfast all the foreign representatives and high dignitaries of the empire.

And now let us listen to what some of our prominent Americans, whose patriotism none can assail, have to say about our present-day observance. First "Mark Twain," in whose heart of hearts the small boy is enshrined, and who certainly would not needlessly curtail even one of his little pleasures. Does he approve of our day of "burning" patriotism? No; for he has written to me:

I am with you sincerely in your crusade against the bedlam frenzies of the Fourth of July.

And William Dean Howells:

I am glad that you have added to your noble and beneficent ambition to suppress all unnecessary noises the wish especially to deal with the barbarous and obstreperous celebration of the Fourth of July. I am sure that Confucius did not invent gunpowder, and that it was not Chinese *wisdom* which gave us firecrackers. Until we cease to glorify our national birthday like a nation of lawless boys we shall have no right to claim that we have come of age, and the civilized world must regard us as savages until we stop behaving like them.

And one of our poets:

It is good news that you are turning your attention to the subject of the irrational manner in which Americans celebrate their independence. I am sure you will not merely advocate the suppression of meaningless noise, and that you will indicate such fêtes, ceremonies, pageants, and celebrations in general as are rational and instructive; also, that you will hint at a broader and more inspiring use of the day than either arousing old and debasing international enmities or the display of indecent self-glorification.

As to the suppression of Fourth of July noise, with its dangers to nerve, limb, and life, the whole sensible population will wish you a continuance of that success which has followed your efforts on a narrower scale in the metropolis. I am reminded that in the sweet and peaceful valley from which I write the national holiday is looked forward to with apprehension, on account of the dreadful, sleep-scattering noises of the night and dawn before. On the Fourth, why should we not have music instead of noise, art, instead of gunpowder? Every community in the United States will have occasion to bless your name and memory if you can do something substantial toward making more quiet and more ennobling the anniversary of the day that gave the Republic birth.

Here, too, is a letter from Dr. Weir Mitchell:

If anything can be done to lessen the noise of the Fourth of July celebrations, it will also be efficient in lessening the amount of injuries inflicted by the desire of man and boy to make meaningless noises. Not only does it leave the Fourth of July as an annually recurrent unpleasant memory, but there is the same absurd tendency to extend the nuisance of noises into other days. Thus at present in this city, and I presume elsewhere, the first of the year is ushered in by a vast chorus of idiotic noises produced by steam-whistles, firecrackers, and horns, accompanied by a solemn bell-ringing, such as in old times called those who watched for the coming of the New Year to prayer.

That our Commissioner of Health fully recognizes the necessity of bringing about a saner mode of celebration is shown by the following letter:

Your plan to include, as part of the activities of the Society for the Suppression of Unnecessary Noise, the question of a more sensible celebration of the Fourth of July, meets with my most hearty approval. The long list of killed and wounded, which comes as the result of what should be a day of patriotic inspiration, is certainly appalling, and indicative of how far we have strayed from its true spirit.

Your efforts to induce the people of this country to

celebrate its most joyous anniversary in a manner fitting and appropriate, provide an object which should enlist the sympathy and coöperation of all who have the welfare of their country at heart.

And finally . . . I offer this letter from the Hon. Henry L. West, Commissioner of the District of Columbia, which shows that even officialdom is willing to risk the charge of lack of patriotism, if by so doing our boys and girls may be saved from the horrors of a day of catastrophes:

I am thoroughly in sympathy with any movement which will result in decreasing the habit of carelessly using gunpowder on the Fourth of July and which will also result in a more quiet celebration of the day.

In Washington the authorities have already taken a step in the right direction in forbidding the explosion of the so-called giant firecrackers, nor is it allowable to place torpedoes on the street railway tracks.

I believe that the Fourth of July can be celebrated with as much patriotism and more sanity if the wanton use of gunpowder on that day is condemned.

And now, before taking up the question of what might be suggested as a more reverent and appropriate mode of honoring our day of days, let us look back a hundred years or so, and see how our first national birthdays were kept. Here it is encouraging to learn that nothing resembling in the least our wild orgy of noise was dreamed of. Indeed, had such a suggestion been breathed to the sons and daughters of our Revolutionary heroes, they would probably have felt that the plan savored more of China, the land of noise and the home of the firecracker, than of their own country, and have been profoundly shocked at the mere idea that such an anniversary could receive so murderous a recognition. A glance over the time-yellowed pages of the *Evening Post,* printed more than a century ago, or those of the *New York Packet,* which was old when the *Post* was young, shows how differently the Fourth was observed by those who had seen burst into full flower that glorious patriotism which had given it birth. The proclamations, announcements, poems, and advertisements which appeared in those July days of long ago are touching in their patriotic, though grandiloquent, fervor. Here, for instance, is a bit from an announcement of the Tammany Association which appeared in the " Season of Fruit, Year of the Discovery, 310 " (July 1):

Brothers. This Day, like the Sun which illuminates it, sheds a bright and diffusive luster, and welcomes all to partake of its radiance. Once it witnessed the blood-stained field, the plundered town, the ravaged coast, the sinking warrior, the defenseless town, the despondency of our Guardian Genius. But the Great Spirit watched over the western clime, and now its approach is hailed with the incense of Peace; and the veteran rejoices in his scars, the hoary chief and his patriot sons assemble with congratulations where once the noise of battle was heard, and the Eagle towers aloft majestic and unawed.

In these days the celebration began with unfurling the flag, a salute of thirteen guns and ringing of church-bells, followed by a procession and exchange of courtesies between the Governor and the President. Then came the march to church, where odes, addresses, anthems, and orations were in order with, of course, the reading of the Declaration of Independence. Next, luncheon, with more salutes and bell-ringing and then, evening having come, performances in theaters and gardens and the meeting of various patriotic societies. Everything connected with the performances was patriotically reminiscent. In the gardens, transparencies and fireworks portrayed temples of immortality, obelisks of heroes, and figures of Justice, Fidelity, Fame, and Piety, all radiantly intermingled with shining pictures of Washington and of the Arms of the United States, with its brilliant stars, while at the theater, patriotic plays were given, such as "Bunker Hill" or the "Death of Warren and the Glory of Columbia" or the "Retrospect of the American Revolution." This all refers to New York, but it is probable that virtually the same observance obtained in other large cities.

Let us now consider what might be substituted for our present-day mad and dangerous celebration, which serves only to keep in remembrance one feature of our great struggle, the cannonading and musketry-discharges which shook the country during the arduous days of its birth. I sincerely believe that our national birthday can be observed with heartfelt patriotic rejoicing, and yet without the slightest danger to life or limb, without any nerve-racking noise or display of hoodlumism, and without any of the extravagant outlay which has characterized our former celebrations. Flags can float, national music be played and sung in places now given over solely to the deafening din of cannon firecrackers, the Declaration of Independence be read at all of our public buildings, where inspiring addresses may also be made, and street-displays, such as processions with floats, beautiful as well as instructive, furnish delightful object-lessons of the greatest events in our history. Then, at night, we may have illuminations, both private and municipal, and displays of fireworks in open places, where the exhibitions can be conducted by experienced men, thus avoiding all danger of the shocking accidents which now sadden our celebration. Let us, on this day, forget the noise of battle and the passions of international strife, and remember only the wonderful spirit of sacrifice, and patriotism, and brotherhood which animated our Revolutionary heroes. Let us, who know what the day means, endeavor to make it both memorable and illuminating to those who do not, by opening the hearts of the children, of the poor and ignorant, of the distressed and disheartened alien within our gates, to at least a partial significance of what we honor in our glorious festival. Let us enter personally into the work, giving tender endeavor as well as means to the task of making the occasion the happiest of all the year to the ignorant and the wretched. Let us give them a day of liberty in the country or in the parks, where they will see our beautiful flag floating everywhere about them, and where their untrained ears will become accustomed to the ringing rhythm of our national melodies. Let us give them mementos of the Fourth, such as flags and pictures of our heroes and of those whom we love as well as honor. There let them listen to the story of the birth of our Republic, and have it told simply and, if necessary, in their own tongues, so that all can feel how great were those who made the country free, and how wonderful is the boon of liberty now extended to the oppressed of other countries.

A SAFE AND SANE FOURTH OF JULY

BY HENRY LITCHFIELD WEST

(From *The Forum*, August, 1909.)

A LITTLE more than a year ago the *Century Magazine* contained a vigorous and convincing article by Mrs. Isaac L. Rice, entitled " Our Barbarous Fourth." It was a protest against a condition of affairs in the United States which had long attracted attention but which no one, up to that time, had criticised in such emphatic terms. " The grim statistics of the Fourth of July," said the article, " probably furnish a sadder commentary of human folly than that afforded by any other celebration in the world." . . .

It is true that a few thoughtful people had in more or less nonchalant manner observed the terrible toll of death and injury which the evil celebration of the day demanded. Quite a number of newspapers — notably the *Chicago Tribune* — were questioning the wisdom of a method which in one day had resulted in the death of 164 people, and the injury of nearly 5,000. " How can any satisfaction," asked the *New York Tribune,* " be taken in the perversion of a holiday to purposes of disorder and destruction, and how can any pride be felt in methods of observance which inevitably condemn hundreds — if not thousands — to be shot, burned, maimed, and otherwise disfigured and tortured in propitiation of the great god of senseless uproar? " The *St. Paul Pioneer Press* deplored the fact that a day which ought to be the most enjoyable in the calendar had become a day of general carnage;

while the *New York Commercial* characterized the popular celebration as ridiculous and senseless.

Notwithstanding these occasional utterances of truth, which indicated a growing sentiment, the fact is, that at the time of the appearance of " Our Barbarous Fourth " there was only one city in the country wherein any curb had been placed upon the insensate and reckless custom of observing the Fourth of July with dynamite and gunpowder. The cemeteries and the hospitals were claiming their victims and yet no one in authority seemed courageous enough to call a halt for fear of being charged with lack of patriotism. I believe, however, that the article in question appeared at the psychological moment. It was so straightforward in its presentation of the facts, so earnest in its appeal and so logical in its assertion that there were numerous sensible ways of celebrating our national holiday, that it made a profound impression everywhere. At any rate, the fact is, that before that article appeared only one city in the country had prohibited the sale and explosion of fireworks, while within a short period after it had been printed the authorities in several cities took radical action along the lines therein suggested. It is no exaggeration to say that within the next ten years the old barbarous Fourth of July will have entirely disappeared, and it is also within the bounds of accurate statement to add that the one greatest individual factor in accomplishing the much-needed reform is the author of the *Century* article.

All this is by way of preface to the fact that the experiment of a safe and sane Fourth of July was tried this year in the National Capital; and in the belief that its details will prove of general interest, they are herewith recorded. If, as now seems to be the case, we are on the verge of a revolution in the customs which have been in vogue for half a century, the methods by which the change is to be accomplished are not without their value and significance.

The celebration of the national holiday in the capital a year ago had been marked by so many accidents and fires that some protest against the indiscriminate use of fireworks was uttered, and the Commissioners who govern the city declared themselves in published interviews in favor of a safer and saner observance of the day. No definite action was taken, however, until last November, when the question became acute because hundreds of dealers in fireworks in the city were naturally anxious to know whether they would be permitted to handle explosives. Inquiry of other cities brought forth the fact that Cleveland had already enacted an ordinance forbidding the sale and discharge of fireworks, and a copy of this ordinance was secured. In Washington, as ought to be generally known, there is no common council or board of aldermen, but all regulations governing the municipality are promulgated by the three Commissioners under authority delegated to them by Congress. The question whether Washington should undertake the experiment of a non-explosive Fourth rested, therefore, with these three men, and it did not take them long to reach their conclusion. One of them had, more than a year previously, formally expressed his sympathy with the object sought to be attained by the opponents of the barbarous Fourth, and his colleagues were, happily, of the same opinion. In November, therefore, eight months before the arrival of the holiday, the following regulation was enacted:

" No firecracker, squib, or other fireworks of any kind shall be sold and delivered, discharged or set off within the city of Washington, or the fire limits of the District of Columbia, or in the more densely populated portions of said District; provided, however, on occasions of public celebration and exhibition fireworks may be discharged or set off on special permits issued by the Commissioners defining the time, place, storage and such other conditions to be observed in reference thereto as they may deem necessary to the public safety. No gun, air gun, rifle, air rifle, pistol, revolver, or other firearm, cannon or torpedo shall be discharged or set off within the city of Washington, or the fire limits of the District of Columbia, without a special written permit therefor from the Major and Superintendent of Police, nor within five hundred yards of the Potomac River, Eastern Branch, or Anacostia River, Rock Creek, or any public road, highway, schoolhouse, building or buildings, shed, barn, outhouse, public park, reservation, graveyard or burial place, playground, golf course, tennis court, picnic ground, camp ground, or any place where people are accustomed to congregate, inclosure for stock, railroad track, outside of such fire limits for the District of Columbia, without the written consent of the owner or occupant thereof and a special written permit from the Major and Superintendent of Police."

No law or regulation can, however, be effective unless it is sustained by public sentiment. The Commissioners were fortunate in securing the voluntary and enthusiastic support of the members of the Board of Trade and the Chamber of Commerce, the representative local organizations, and, in general, the citizenship of the capital was favorably disposed to the new order of things. Committees were formed for the purpose of providing two patriotic public entertainments, one in the morning to consist of the reading of the Declaration of Independence and appropriate addresses, and the other to include a fine display of fireworks at night upon the ellipse south of the White House. The funds for the latter were promptly supplied by public subscription, and the affair was managed most successfully by a volunteer committee, no less than forty thousand people witnessing the display. In the meantime, the residents of various sections of the District undertook to uphold sympathetically the Commissioners by devising their own collective celebrations. In Cleveland Park, an attractive suburban district, there was a public meeting with a programme of fireworks handled by experts, while Bloomingdale, another well-settled section, enjoyed a day of athletic sports, speeches and aerial fireworks. In short, the people of the District of Columbia cheerfully accepted the proclamation, which was issued by the Commissioners, inviting attention to the police regulations which had been adopted " to provide against the dangers incident to the manner of observing the Fourth of July and Christmas, which previously prevailed," and appealing " to the people of the District of Columbia heartily to second their efforts by observing and counseling the observance of these regulations."

Nor were the entertainments already mentioned the only forms of celebration. The *Washington Post* conceived the idea of an automobile floral-flag parade, and this event proved to be a genuine spectacular and artistic success. There were over a hundred motor cars in line, and the decorations were extremely novel and pleasing. One automobile was reconstructed into an accurate representation of the Confederate ram *Merrimac,* and was manned by young men in sailor costumes; another was converted into a yacht with masts and sails; another was a floral boat apparently drawn by an enormous white swan; and still another was in the form of a pergola, decorated with wistaria vines and blossoms. An electric machine which elicited the applause of the thousands who lined the route of parade was apparently a huge wicker basket of pink roses, in the center of which and surmounted by a canopy of roses was seated the lady who operated the car. Another electric machine was a symphony in red, white and blue. Altogether, the event proved to be a most unique and beautiful celebration, and the committee of artists who awarded the cups and other prizes, valued at $1,500, was confronted by a most difficult task of selection. When it is considered that the affair was the first of its kind in the National Capital, and was merely suggested as one form of rational enjoyment, its successful execution occasioned deserved felicitation, and when it is repeated next year, as it will be, the national holiday will be made literally a day of delight.

The real value, however, of the experiment in the National Capital still remains to be recorded. Instead of a long list of dead and injured, there was not a single gunpowder accident in the city, and the two minor alarms of fire were not occasioned by explosives. The contrast between the recent Fourth of July celebration and those of previous years, is strikingly shown in the following figures:

Number of persons treated at local hospitals for injuries from explosives:

HOSPITAL.	July 4, 1908.	July 5, 1909.
Emergency	25	0
Casualty	6	0
Freedmen's	5	0
Georgetown	10	0
Providence	0	0
Homeopathic	52	0
Children's	2	0
Totals	104	0

Before the Fourth there was some division of opinion as to the outcome; after the Fourth the public sentiment was practically unanimous as to the humanity and wisdom of a safe and sane celebration. This sentiment found editorial expression in the daily newspapers, and those communities which are considering the advisability of abolishing the dangerous customs of the past, might with great profit read these comments. They are here incorporated almost in their entirety:

Washington Herald:

Having celebrated the Fourth of July in a safe and sane manner, it is reasonably sure that Washington will not hereafter entertain the thought of going back to the stereotyped, unsafe, and insane way of observing the anniversary of the country's independence. It is true that the day, for the most part, was so quiet as to be almost Sabbathlike; but, thanks to an ideally delightful spell of weather, every hour, from dawn until the night festivities concluded, was full of wholesome enjoyment. A welcome relief it was, indeed, to be spared the affliction of the ear-splitting firecracker and toy cannon nuisance and kindred evils that made other Fourths so hideous. And a more welcome relief still is the knowledge to-day that Washington, at least, has not a long hospital list of maimed and suffering victims of the reckless use of explosives.

Washington Times:

On the day following the Fourth, it will be difficult to find many people who will not give their approval to the innovation. Nobody's home was burned up, nobody succeeded in killing himself or his neighbor; there are no incipient cases of lockjaw under observation. The tendency to those other forms of disorder which grow out of indulgence in the cup that cheers — and perhaps deafens — was less marked than ever before. The police and the hospitals alike had an easy time of it. Not a single accident worthy the name, of the distinctive variety which has made Independence Day an occasion of carnage and terror, took place in Washington. That is a remarkable record.

Safety and sanity, in short, vindicated themselves to perfection. Promiscuous noise was simply impossible because of the strict prohibition of the sale and use of fireworks and other abominations in the racket-making line. Altogether, it was a glorious day, and it is sincerely to be hoped that it will come in similar fashion once per annum, and in time lead people to a cheerful ability honestly to rejoice that their country did attain its freedom.

Papers in unsafe and insane communities please copy.

Washington Star:

After yesterday's experience it is doubtful whether Washington will ever return to the old customs of Independence Day celebrations. The " safe and sane " Fourth idea was carried out in a manner to please practically the entire community, to give some form of entertainment to the greatest possible number throughout the day, without contributing a single accident of any kind to the records.

Taken in detail, yesterday's celebration features were calculated to please all classes. For those who wished to dwell seriously upon the patriotic aspect of the occasion there was the open-air meeting, where exercises appropriate to the day were held. For the children there was no lack of amusement, with the daylight fireworks diverting them on three different occasions. The floral automobile parade was a novelty that drew large numbers to the line, while the day was appropriately closed with an exceptional exhibition of fireworks, concluding with the illumination of Pennsylvania Avenue.

An ideal day in overhead conditions, yesterday afforded the best opportunity to try the new idea of Independence Day celebration. In consequence of all the arrangements and restrictions there was a remarkable lack of noise from morning till night. There were no fires and the hospital ambulance was less busy even than on ordinary occasions. The policemen had an easy time, being occupied chiefly in preserving lines at the various points of congregation. There was a noteworthy lack of public intoxication. In short, Washington demonstrated that it can enjoy itself in a dignified, decent manner.

With the experience of yesterday in mind, the authorities and citizens who engage in such enterprises can proceed next year to organize an Independence Day celebration that will be even better. It has been proved that it is possible to stop the promiscuous discharge of firecrackers and other forms of explosives. This is in itself an immense advantage. There is no reason to doubt the ability of the Commissioners to maintain order in the same manner next year. It may be suggested that the 1910 programme should include more public music of a patriotic character at intervals during the day and that the chief feature of the occasion be some form of historic pageant.

In the face of this splendid and sensible record, it is appalling to read the reports from other cities. The death of Arthur Granville Langham, uncle of the Baroness von Sternberg, which occurred in Louisville, as the result of the explosion of a cannon cracker, was especially tragic, but the occurrences in other municipalities are none the less sad because the victims were not as prominent in social and financial circles. Here are some of the figures:

NEW YORK. Five killed, 197 injured by fireworks, 82 injured by pistols, 23 injured by cannons and 3 injured by torpedoes; also, 116 fires started by explosives. Notwithstanding this list of victims, one of the most prominent New York papers remarked that New York had broken all records for a safe and sane Fourth of July.

PHILADELPHIA. Five dead, 3 fatally injured, 8 seriously injured and 420 painfully injured; 80 fires.

ST. LOUIS. Four dead, 205 injured.

WILKESBARRE, PA. Four dead.

PITTSBURG. One dead, 295 injured; fire loss, $50,000.

MEMPHIS, TENN. A crippled newsboy burned to death.

WHEELING, W. VA. One dead, 50 injured.

BUFFALO. Fifteen children injured, 40 fires.

BOSTON. One hundred and ten persons injured.

TOLEDO. Boy's left hand necessarily amputated and a fifteen-year-old boy blinded for life.

KANSAS CITY. One death from lockjaw.

ELMIRA, N. Y. Two deaths from lockjaw.

WOONSOCKET, R. I. One dead and a dozen persons injured.

Other cities, without regard to section, afford a painful repetition of casualty. It seems strange that this annual holocaust should be tolerated. There is not a civilized country in the world which pays such a fearful debt to alleged patriotism as the United States. There is no question as to the devotion of the Japanese to their country, and yet their three national holidays are not marred by sad fatalities. Germany celebrates the Emperor's birthday with the greatest enthusiasm, but without wholesale death and injury. France is patriotic, and yet France observes its festal days in a safe and sane fashion. In the City of Mexico, as the writer knows by personal experience, the celebration of Independence Day is a great popular success, and yet not one firecracker is exploded. The experiment in Washington demonstrates that dynamite and gunpowder are not essential to a thorough and patriotic enjoyment of the day. Surely the time will come when other cities will appreciate the importance of celebrating in some manner which will appropriately mark the day, and yet not leave a sanguinary trail of dead and wounded.

It goes without saying that the safe and sane method will not be departed from in the National Capital. In that city, at least, there will be an example of common sense which other municipalities might well emulate. There will be ample opportunity for the expression of patriotic sentiment, unaccompanied by death and disaster, and in less than a decade the people will look back to the ancient and barbarous customs, and wonder how they were ever tolerated for a single hour. Next year new methods of entertainment will be devised, and more consideration will be given to the children. This year the pupils of the public schools sang patriotic songs at the various gatherings, and the children enjoyed the automobile parade and the fireworks. The Fourth of July, however, is essentially Young America's day, and in any programme arranged by a municipality especial consideration should be given to the little ones. With this detail not overlooked, there will be no question of the real success of any Fourth of July celebration. Certainly the experiment which the National Capital has successfully inaugurated has proven worth while; and if the example is generally followed by other cities, there will be safety and sanity everywhere, nor need the splendid fervency of our full-blooded patriotism suffer loss.

THE NEW INDEPENDENCE DAY

BY HENRY B. F. MACFARLAND AND RICHARD B. WATROUS

(As Observed at Washington, D. C., 1909.)

THE programme for the day provided for a display of daylight fireworks at 7th and Pennsylvania Avenue, a central point with park surroundings and no nearby residences, from 9:30 until 10:30 in the morning; then the public meeting at the same place, surrounding the new memorial of the Grand Army of the Republic and its founder, Dr. Stephenson, where Senator Owen, of Oklahoma, made an oration, the Declaration of Independence was read, the " Star Spangled Banner " and " My Country, 'Tis of Thee " were sung, and the school children sang other patriotic songs, and the United States Marine Band volunteered and gave music. After this there was another display of daylight fireworks. At least 5,000 people, chiefly in family groups, attended the meeting and saw these fireworks exhibitions, and the children were delighted with the shows new to Washington. At half past two in the afternoon on the great ellipse south of the White House, at least 10,000 men, women and children listened to a band concert and watched another hour's exhibition of the daylight fireworks, the grown-ups enjoying, as much as the children, the flags, balloons, paper animals, birds and fishes, liberated by the bombs high in air. Later in the afternoon a fine parade of automobiles decorated with flags and flowers, and arranged by the *Washington Post,* and for which it gave most of the prizes, passed up and down Pennsylvania Avenue, crowded by spectators, and around the Capitol and White House and down to Potomac Park where the judges awarded the prizes. In the evening there was an elaborate display of fireworks on the ellipse south of the White House, followed by a beautiful illumination of Pennsylvania Avenue. The newspapers estimated that between 40,000 and 50,000 people saw these night exhibitions. Never was there a more cheerful or good-tempered crowd. Apparently the young and old thoroughly enjoyed the whole day which had a picnic character for most of them. Several of the suburban communities organized their own fireworks exhibitions and some had public meetings as well.

The experience of the day suggested additions and improvements for the celebration of the next Independence Day. Historical pageants, a regatta, more field sports, more band concerts, and a wider distribution of the celebration points are among the things suggested for next year. The Joint Committee on Arrangements has already taken steps to provide a permanent organization to prepare for future celebrations, the Commissioners having announced at once that there will be no repeal or amendment of the regulation prohibiting the old barbaric methods of celebrating the day.   The new order of things met the approval of President Taft who, upon being told by the Chairman of the Joint Committee, the plans for the celebration, wrote the following letter, which was read at the public meeting:

THE WHITE HOUSE, WASHINGTON, July 3, 1909.

My Dear Mr. Macfarland:

I have your letter of July 1st with respect to the celebration of the Fourth of July. I am very sorry that I shall not be in the city on that day because of a previous engagement; but I am heartily in sympathy with the movement to rid the celebration of our country's natal day of those distressing accidents that might be avoided and are merely due to a recklessness against which the public protest cannot be too emphatic.

Very sincerely yours,

(Signed) WM. H. TAFT.

Hon. Henry B. F. Macfarland,
Commissioner of the District of Columbia.

This letter, sent out by the Press Association with a brief account of the celebration, must have helped the cause of the " safe and sane " celebration of Independence Day everywhere.

NEW FOURTHS FOR OLD

BY MRS. ISAAC L. RICE

" When you are past shrieking, having no human articulate voice to say you are glad with, you fill the quietude . . . with gunpowder blasts, and rush home, red with cutaneous eruption of conceit and voluble with convulsive hiccough of self-satisfaction. . . . It is pitiful to have dim conceptions of duty; more pitiful, it seems to me, to have conceptions like these of mirth."— *John Ruskin.*

WHEN the preparations for the celebration of a great anniversary are identical with those for a battle, it is time to pause and reflect whether a better observance of the day might not be advisable — to ask ourselves whether one might not be planned which would honor and not dishonor a glorious memory.

When Physicians, Boards of Health and Hospital Superintendents annually prepare for the reception and treatment of hundreds, or rather thousands, who will — before the close of the day — be brought in torn, burned, blinded; when undertakers prepare for the hideous aftermath of our National Birthday; when hundreds of thousands of the sick look forward with dread to the recurrence of this season of noise, which to them brings so much distress; when fathers and mothers all over the country shudder at the thought of what the Fourth may bring to their dear ones, I believe that one is justified in characterizing as a national disgrace that pseudo-patriotism which is responsible for so much agony.

It is impossible to exaggerate the stigma of shame incurred by the intelligent, adult proportion of the population in deliberately and scientifically prepar-

ing for the massacre and maiming of the youthful,
ignorant and heedless members of the community.
One city, for instance, added twenty-six surgeons to
its ambulance corps, while another engaged twelve dis-
tributors of tetanus antitoxin, had field dressing
stations prepared by its National Volunteer Emergency
Service and sent around fifteen hundred vials of antitoxin serum to its hospitals. And thus many cities
anticipated the return of their Day of Carnage, pre-
paring to bind wounds and lacking the courage required to insist on the passage of drastic prohibitive
ordinances which would have rendered impossible the
shedding of blood.

I am sure that the thanks of all are due to one of
our medical publications which, for years past, has
compiled statistics upon statistics, based upon the price
that we pay for our present-day mad celebration of
the Fourth, for without the splendid work of the
Journal of the American Medical Association we
should be unable to estimate the cost of our annual
holiday. As for the figures, so laboriously compiled,
they are simply amazing. To think of fifteen hundred
and thirty-one deaths and thirty-three thousand and
seventy-three accidents, the fearful sacrifice voluntarily
offered by us, within the last seven years, to our false
ideals! And yet these tables, shocking as they are,
give so inadequate an idea of the suffering involved!
For of these fifteen hundred and thirty-one deaths,
practically none came painlessly, almost all being accompanied by the convulsions of tetanus, the torments
of fire, or the shock of injuries which changed healthy,
happy children into shapeless, agonizing horrors.
While as for the thirty-three thousand and seventy-
three who were injured, but not fatally, how many are

dragging out their wretched lives, blind, maimed or crippled!

What, perhaps, is the saddest feature, is the fact that almost all the victims of the Fourth are children, whose youth and ignorance and inexperience and helplessness would certainly seem to merit all due protection at our hands. Poor little ones, who play delightedly with danger! And then how many among the victims of the Fourth are those who have not been "celebrating," but who have been shot down or burnt to death by the wanton recklessness of Independence Day "Patriots" (God save the mark!). Bullets, cannon-crackers, blank cartridges, and strings of Chinese crackers spare none. Little babes have had their heads torn open, mothers have been killed as they sat beside their children, scores of girls have been burnt to death by having lighted firecrackers or fireworks thrown in their direction. Runaways have been frequent because hoodlums love to throw great "bombs" under frightened teams, and one of the merriest sports has been to place large torpedoes on car-tracks. In Vincennes (Indiana), for instance, one Fourth was "celebrated" by placing boxes of explosives on the tracks, by means of which car windows were shattered, passengers terrified and injured, and traffic blocked for hours; after these boxes had all been picked up it was found that two barrels of explosives had been collected. In Boston, only two years ago, seventy arrests were made for using firearms, while in Pittsburg a party of rich, young hoodlums terrorized the holiday crowds by dashing along in an automobile, firing volleys of shots up and down the streets and into the shops. Pittsburg's arrests July 4, 1907, numbered 300. But, then, what can we expect when we repeal for a period of twenty-four hours almost all laws regarding safety and sanity?

As for the licensed recklessness, responsible for so many accidents, the recital of some of the mad acts to which it has led in the past is simply incredible. Some of these acts were: the throwing of dynamite bombs and giant crackers and the firing of revolvers into holiday crowds, the tossing of lighted firecrackers into the laps, or against the thin clothing, of women and girls, resulting in their being roasted to death; the filling of pipes and tin cans with dynamite, or the stuffing of bottles with lighted firecrackers — all with inevitable consequences. These are but a few of the acts which caused these 33,073 accidents, but the excuse for all was always the same — Patriotism! If this, however, is Patriotism, then it recalls — with but a slight variation as to meaning — that utterance of Dr. Johnson's: "Patriotism which is the last refuge of the scoundrel." However, it is not Patriotism, but only craving for noise and excitement and danger which kills and blinds and maims on our Day of Carnage. Some, indeed, go so far as to declare that the usual celebration of the Fourth is "due to desire to break loose into a day of savagery and wallow in the unusual." Perhaps, if a stop is not soon put to this mad orgy, we shall find ourselves changing the words of our National Anthem, as suggested by one of our dailies, and singing:

"My country, 'Tis of Thee,
For Thou hast Crippled Me."

However, it is not Patriotism but Hoodlumism and the desire to revel in a day from which all sane and safe restrictions have been removed, which may be said to guide most of the celebrants on the Fourth, for most of them are undoubtedly ignorant of its glorious significance. That this is true was amusingly shown in one of our large eastern cities where between thirty and forty thousand children were asked in the public schools why they celebrated the Fourth of July. The favorite answer was said to have been " For shoots," others were: " For a band," " For chicken to eat," and most astounding of all " For the King of the Jews " (the similarity of sound between Jew and July doubtless suggesting the last).

The duration of our " noise-fest " varies in different localities, in some being limited to a few hours, in others being permitted to extend over several weeks. Where this premature celebration is allowed, it naturally entails great suffering on the sick, not to speak of the additional danger incurred by the youthful participants. It is this early start which, doubtless, prompted the remark: " The Fourth of July is the only holiday which begins before it happens." As for the celebration proper, it generally starts on the evening of the third and lasts until the morning or the afternoon of the fifth. In some cities, however, it does not begin until midnight, in others not until four o'clock in the morning. However, even where the noisy period is the shortest, the suffering borne by our hospital patients is sufficient to excite the sympathy of all those with whom they come in contact.

Regarding the monetary cost of our celebration, New York City is reported to have spent about $14,-000,000 on the celebration of two holidays, with a resultant loss of 11 persons killed and 768 injured. As for the total monetary loss to the whole country, it can scarcely be calculated, nor can the fire-loss be estimated. Regarding the latter, however, I have been enabled, through the courtesy of Mr. Miller, General Agent of the National Board of Fire Underwriters, to obtain a few figures which show that during five years (from 1898 to 1902 inclusive) there were 4,827 fires in the United States due to fireworks; in Massachusetts from 1902 to 1906 inclusive there were 278 fires due to the same cause; and in Boston in one year, 1906, 72 took place. But quite apart from the effect of these conflagrations on our fire-loss (which is about nine times as high as that of the chief countries of Europe — $3 per capita as against 33 cents), many accidents might perhaps be traced to carelessness engendered in the young by the annually repeated spectacle of a whole community playing with fire and explosives. I firmly believe that this one day of dangerous license exerts a pernicious effect upon the other three hundred and sixty-four days of the year.

An example of what an enthusiastically patriotic and yet sane and safe holiday observance can be, was given last May, when England and her colonies celebrated "Empire Day." This fête was observed by tens of millions, scattered over one-fourth of the world's surface, and yet not one death was reported — not a single accident marred the glory and the happiness of the day. In this splendid world-pageant, the citizens of to-morrow were the chief actors, and it is estimated that fully eight millions took part. Children in long procession, thousands of them in uniform, wearing flags on their breasts and carrying them aloft in an endless blaze of color, marched along to render homage to the Union Jack, which fluttered out above their heads as the little soldiers were reviewed, or as they sang the National Anthem. The floral emblems of the day was the daisy or, failing that, the bachelor's button, marigold or marguerite — the watchwords were " Responsibility, duty, sympathy, self-sacrifice." In addition to the National Anthem, Rudyard Kipling's " Children's Song " was also sung by millions of little ones:

> " Lord of our birth, our faith, our pride,
> For whose dear sake our Fathers died,
> O, Motherland, we pledge to thee
> Head, heart and hand through years to be."

As for France, everybody knows how joyfully it enters upon the celebration of its Day of Liberation, July 14th. Military reviews, artistically beautiful street decoration, free theatrical and operatic performances, music, splendid displays of fireworks from the bridges, and public dancing in the streets and squares, make up a day of happy and sane observance — a huge kermess. Perhaps no other country celebrates its birthday with quite the same stern simplicity, the same touching faith as Switzerland, when on August 1st, no outward manifestation of the national thanksgiving is remarked, except in the ringing of bells and the blazing of bonfires on the mountain peaks, or in the singing of a few inspiring songs. The whole nation seems to be listening to the voices of the past, while continuing its daily tasks, this sturdy band of mountaineers! And thus with the celebrations of yet more European countries, Germany, Sweden, Denmark and still others, everything is marked by sanity and order, and yet by true thanksgiving and joy.

But although the American abroad may well blush with shame in comparing our " Horrible Fourth," our " Tetanus Day," our " Annual Massacre," our " Modern Massacre of Innocents," our " Carnival of Lockjaw," our " Bloody Fourth," or our " Day of Carnage," with the fête days of other lands, let him take courage, for at last it really seems as if " Explosive Patriotism " were " on the run." Throughout the Union, scores of cities have already passed or are considering the passage of restrictive or, better still, of prohibitive ordinances, and countless organizations are getting into line in their efforts to substitute attractive features, such as children's processions and merry-making, pageantry, musical festivals, picnics, and other safe observances for our present orgy of death. In order to show at a glance what has already been gained by legislation in preventing Fourth of July accidents, let us place side by side the results obtained a few months ago in two groups of cities. In the first let us put Washington, Cleveland, Baltimore and Toledo, which cities protected by prohibitive or restrictive ordinances, gave last Fourth of July a total of twelve accidents. The other four, New York, Philadelphia, Boston and St. Louis, which were all relatively unprotected, gave a total of thirteen hundred and ninety-seven accidents, or an average of almost three hundred and fifty apiece. Drastic ordinances and stern enforcement are required if we are ever to down our National Disgrace.

Let us protect our little ones from death and danger, and then the next step will be to learn to express " social ideals in action," for as Mr. Luther Gulick so well says: " If there is any one thing, any one occasion, in connection with which there should be national community expression, it should be in connection with our celebration of American independence. This constitutes not only the pivotal point in the history of American institutions, but is the pivotal idea upon which democracy rests."

Nothing is more inspiring than love of country, therefore let us advocate a " religion of patriotism " and do away with a false death-dealing patriotism which, annually, on our National Birthday disgraces us in the eyes of the whole civilized world.

AMERICANIZING THE FOURTH

(A Suggestion for a Pageant of Liberty.)

BY ROBERT HAVEN SCHAUFFLER

The old, undemocratic idea of honoring the birthday of American independence is embodied in annual explosions of barbarism which have already done to death many more persons than the Revolutionary War destroyed. Indeed, our peaceful celebration seems as much more dangerous than the old style of warfare as small-pox is more dangerous than chicken-pox.

Our new festival in honor of Liberty is — or is soon to be — very different. Instead of a day of pseudo-patriotism,— a - Moloch-day sacred to blinding and maiming our little ones, to shredding and roasting them alive, blowing them to bits or allowing them to struggle to their death in the horrible clutch of tetanus — there is proposed a day of the deepest, fairest, most enthusiastic, most genuine patriotism; a day of emphasis not upon erratic individualism but upon national solidarity; a day of fun yet of education and inspiration to old as well as young and to all the nations that are now being fused in our gigantic melting pot. In a word, the new movement aims, as it should, to make the Fourth our most profoundly *American* holiday.

The recent rise of the Independence Day pageant is a by-product of two wide twentieth century movements: the new classicism and the new democracy. The new classicism is behind the current tendency of certain of the arts to react from the rich, vague elaboration of an exaggerated romanticism toward plain, clearly organized simplicity. In a word, it is trying to restore a normal balance between the emotional and the intellectual elements in art. In music this movement is led by Max Reger, the modern Bach; in architecture it is felt in the *Art Nouveau* and, in America, in such significant buildings as the New York Library and the Pennsylvania Terminal; in literature in the recent rebirth of the drama, of which the pageant is a near relative. For the pageant has been defined as " a dramatic presentation of the history of a community or of the development of a phase of civilization, given by the people themselves."

The movement called the new democracy is slightly older. Under President Roosevelt this country discovered a new and more vital meaning in the old term " democracy." And it has not taken us long to find out that on Independence Day the square deal is less thrillingly symbolized by the maiming and slaughter of innocent thousands through the meaningless cracker and pistol than by the coöperation of all nationalities and social grades on our shores in great, concerted movements, large with the meaning of the past, the present and the future America, and glowing with the local colors of the many peoples that have made and are to make this nation.

The inevitable medium for such expression is the pageant. And though this form of celebration is still in its early infancy and has not yet attained even the modest measure of clarity already reached in other arts by the new classicism, nor even the puny measure of real democracy exhibited to-day by our "square deal" renaissance, yet it is quite as big with promise as they.

The Pageant of Liberty, which is here proposed, is based on the idea that America was the pioneer in that modern struggle for liberty which has played such a striking part in the world's history since 1776. Our War of Independence inspired the French Revolution which, in turn, brandished the torch of liberty through Europe during the nineteenth century until, in our day, the flame has spread to other continents.

This Pageant consists of a parade of simple floats which may or may not end in a dramatic and choral performance or "masque" in some athletic field or fair ground or stadium. The floats and their costumed characters are to be the actors in this masque.

These floats need not be elaborate or expensive or hard to construct. In most cases all that is required is a plain large truck, festooned with simple garlands, and with the wheels hidden in oak branches. This truck carries the necessary characters, dressed, of course, in the costume of the period.

There need be none of those complicated, elaborately colored, pyramidal structures of "staff" which endangered the success of the Hudson-Fulton Celebration in New York City. For they are difficult and costly to prepare and doubtful of effect. The effect sought should be pictorial rather than sculpturesque. In many cases a single small platform or table is the only " property " required.

The floats in procession represent the history of the modern struggle for liberty. This history, however, may be depicted as fully or as sketchily as the particular resources of each place suggest, each foreign colony in a town working up its own float under central supervision.

In our day most American cities and towns have a large percentage of the foreign born. Let us suppose, for example, that a certain large town consists of the following nine nationalities: Americans, French, Irish, Servians, Germans, Greeks, Hungarians, Italians, and Persians. In that case its particular pageant would consist of at least ten floats, each attended on foot or horseback by its appropriate escort of the same race, preferably in national costume, and by bands of music playing — perhaps on native instruments — those national airs most nearly identified with the particular historical event set forth.

I. THE AMERICAN float will naturally head the procession, for precedence in this pageant is fixed by the historical order in which the various struggles for liberty occurred.

The American float might represent the Fathers sitting about a table and signing the Declaration of Independence, with the Liberty Bell hanging aloft. Or it might be boat-shaped, with Washington in the bow, crossing the Delaware and tattered soldiers straining at the oars or poling away at imaginary ice-cakes.

The other floats would follow in this order:

II. FRANCE. King Louis XVI is forced to recognize General Lafayette, the commander of the new National Guard, on July 17, 1789, and affixes to his own royal garments the tricolor cockade of red, blue and white, the symbol of liberty. This event occurred three days after the storming of the Bastille, a subject that would not lend itself well to pictorial treatment.

III. IRELAND. Some incident from the Rebellion of 1798. The float might be in honor of the patriotic Society of United Irishmen and of their founder, Theobald Wolfe Tone. Or it might represent the dramatic betrayal, on May 19, 1798, of Lord Edward Fitzgerald, the promised leader of the revolt.

IV. SERVIA. Some incident from the splendid rebellion of 1804 when the Serbs, who had been galled by the Ottoman yoke for more than four centuries, rose and drove the Turkish *dahis* out of Servia. Their two leaders were Black George and Milosch who have been called respectively the Achilles and the Ulysses of Servian history. The float might give the crucial moment in the decisive battle of Schabaz, with Black George leading his men against those picturesque standard-bearers of the Turkish army, the bravest Begs of Bosnia.

V. GERMANY. It is not so easy to find a moment in the German struggle which is both significant and simple enough for our purpose. Perhaps the " Wartburg Festival " would answer. Some historians treat this incident in lighter vein, others seriously. But all agree that the government reactionaries took it very much to heart and at once began a reign of tyranny that was largely responsible for the revolutions of '30 and of historic '48. At any rate the Festival would make a most effective float. This was the way it happened.

A couple of years after the battle of Waterloo secret political societies were formed all over Germany among the students and the athletes. These were called the *Burschenschaften* and the Turners. On October 17, 1818, several hundred of these young fellows met at the Wartburg (the ancient castle which had sheltered Luther after he had defied the pope and the emperor). That evening they gathered about a bonfire and fed it with various symbols of despotism and with the effigies of reactionary books, while, hard by, the Turners did exuberant gymnastic " stunts." This float could be made most realistic with a genuine bonfire and a couple of Turners in the rear performing, perhaps, on a horizontal bar. The decorations should be in black, red and yellow, the colors of German liberty.

VI. GREECE. The float might merely show a group of the picturesquely costumed leaders of the Revolution of 1821. There would be General Kolokotrones, Marco Botzaris (the Suliote chieftain immortalized in Fitz-Greene Halleck's poem), Admiral Miaoulis, Kanaris of fire-ship fame, Karaiskakis, the daring guerilla, and Lord Byron, the poet of revolt, who gave his life for the cause, and without whom there might have been no Greek independence.

A more dramatic subject would be found in the Greeks' welcome of Byron when he arrived at Missolonghi in the fall of 1823. The costumes of this float would be particularly effective.

VII. HUNGARY. One turns naturally to the events of April 14, 1849, when, on Kossuth's motion, the diet proclaimed the independence of Hungary. This ought to be as practicable as to give the signing of our own Declaration.

As an alternative scheme, General Görgei could be shown, surrounded by the evidences of some of his victories, such as Szólnok, Isaszeg, Vácz, and Nagysarló.

VIII. ITALY. Italian liberty might well be epitomized in the spectacle of a red-shirted Garibaldi leaning from the balcony of the Foresteria (the balcony could be made out of two packing boxes and a bit of railing) and addressing the jubilant Neapolitans on Sept. 7, 1860, at the close of his conquest of the Two Sicilies.

IX. PERSIA. This unique float would show a handful of the Mujteheds, or higher Mohammedan priests, taking refuge, or "bast" before the shrine of Shah Abdul Azim near Teheran, as they did in 1905. The taking of "bast" in some sanctuary or other place of protection is an old Persian method of political protest. In this case it inaugurated the recent revolution which won Persia a constitution.

X. LIBERTY. The final float would be devoted to displaying the charms of the most statuesquely beautiful young woman in the community,— who would be dressed and accoutered rather like the Statue of Liberty in New York harbor, only, one hopes, with somewhat better taste.

In this order the procession would parade the principal streets. Then, finally it would march to the stadium (or athletic field) for the dramatic part of the pageant, if this part were found desirable.

But before passing to the masque, a few more suggestions must be offered about the parade.

The idea already outlined is capable of almost infinite expansion. For most of the immigrant nations in our country have undergone struggles that were inspired, directly or indirectly, by 1776.

Suppose a town wishes to celebrate its next Fourth with a Liberty Pageant; — it has merely to select an Independence Day Committee as Springfield did. This committee prepares a list of the different local nationalities, and decides on the most important modern struggle for liberty in the history of each, and finally, on the characters or events that will most simply and effectively epitomize that struggle in float form.

A few picturesque Tyrolese, for instance, could make a thrilling picture of the gallant rising of Andreas Hofer in 1809. The Croatians have a spirited picture in the 1849 proclamation of their independence of Hungary. The Poles would find a spirited subject in the rebellion of 1830, which began with a band of brave students trying to seize the Grand Duke Constantine at his palace near Warsaw. Cuba could recall her Declaration of Independence of Oct. 10, 1868, or some event of the late war. Spain could have a Ferrer float. Norway might remind us of her recent bloodless separation from Sweden. Russia, of one of the many dramatic incidents in that long, bitter fight for liberty whose end is not yet in sight.

Not alone by increasing the number of participating nations is this idea capable of almost endless development, but also by increasing the number of floats for each nation. The history of most of the struggles already alluded to contains dozens of alluring subjects. The number need be limited only by the resources and the enthusiasm of the community.

Behind the national floats international ones might

follow, representing such world-movements as those
for:

RELIGIOUS LIBERTY
FREEDOM OF SPEECH
FREEDOM OF THE PRESS
ABOLITION OF SLAVERY
EXTENSION OF THE ELECTIVE FRANCHISE
POPULARIZATION OF GOVERNMENT
DESTRUCTION OF SPECIAL PRIVILEGE
EMANCIPATION OF WOMAN
ABOLITION OF MOB RULE
ABOLITION OF CHILD LABOR
ETC., ETC.

So much, then, for the possibilities of expanding the
idea. On the other hand it is capable of just as extreme contraction and simplification for use in the
smaller, less wealthy communities.

By taking a little more care in costuming the
marching escorts an effective pageant could be arranged with only five or six floats.

Indeed, it is not absolutely essential to have floats
at all. Nearly all of the situations suggested above
could be adequately represented by appropriately costumed groups on foot; and there would even be this
positive advantage, that leaders like Garibaldi and
Kolokotrones and Black George might appear at the
head of a more realistically adequate body of troops
than could be assembled upon a float.

According to this plan the various foes of liberty
might also appear in force, and sham battles could be
fought in various outskirts of town earlier in the day
(let us hope, with noiseless as well as smokeless
arms!) before the various units unite in procession.

If the parade is combined with the performance of a specially written masque, the combination would obviate many of the usual objections to the ordinary "safe and sane" Fourth. The masque would provide a most desirable dramatic and educative element. And, by charging a small admission fee, this performance would ordinarily pay the entire expense of the celebration, including the expense of engaging a competent pageant master. Now a pay performance without the free parade might, under the circumstances, be considered an undemocratic way of celebrating what should be our most democratic holiday. But in combination with a free parade the admission fee would be unobjectionable, and the masque would, more than anything else, stimulate that deep, thoughtful patriotism whose lack to-day is as grave a defect in our barbarous Fourth as its cruelty.

The idea of the masque has as yet been worked out only, tentatively. Its development is the business of a dramatic poet. Roughly speaking it would proceed somewhat as follows.

When the procession arrives at the stadium the floats would enter in their historical order, each accompanied however, by only the small, specially trained nucleus of its marching escort. The floats would circle the inclosure once or twice, and then divide into two files, forming a lane of honor through which the Liberty float would move slowly and take up a position in the center of the inclosure.

Its escort would then sing a chorus which ought to be as eloquent and beautiful and suggestive an exposition of the nature of abstract liberty as Swinburne's "Hertha" is of the soul.

When this is finished the Americans would approach this central figure of Liberty and recount, with music and dramatic action, perhaps, their struggle in her honor, ending with America sung with full chorus and band. Then the Americans would take up their position in the secondary place of honor opposite.

Hereupon, keeping to their historic order, each nation would advance and after greeting the American float as the pioneer of liberty, would approach the goddess and briefly recite their deeds in her behalf, each particularly emphasizing the unique qualities which it brought to its own struggle, and which it is ready (by application) to bring to any further struggles in the same general cause.

These national recitals might be managed in various ways. Dependent upon the size of the stadium and the available creative talent among the organizers, they might be spoken or sung, solo or in chorus, in prose or verse, or both. Of course it is desirable that the masque should be composed entirely by the best poet and set to music by the most inspired composer obtainable. But it is quite conceivable that local amateurs might rise to very satisfactory heights in an emergency.

Even in case of rain it might still be possible for the leading characters to present this masque upon the stage of the largest local theater concert hall.

After each nation has separately recounted its prowess, and all are grouped effectively around the central figure, Liberty reminds them that though they have done heroic deeds in the past, much remains to accomplish in the present, even in this land of the free. She then proceeds to describe what foes still menace our real freedom in America, such foes as special privilege, mob rule, political corruption, white slavery, treatment of the feeble-minded as common criminals, a capitalistic press, and so on.

Then in the final grand chorus the united nations would join together in proclaiming that, strengthened by their separate struggles overseas, they here and now unite their efforts to make this land, in deed as in name, the land of liberty.

Could anything make more swiftly and surely for national solidarity than in some such way to stimulate each national element in our forming civilization to bring the best it has to the service of the future America? And what more patriotic and fitting deed could be accomplished than to transform the birth-day of modern liberty from a day of meaningless destruction into a day of construction fraught with profound and beautiful significance?

THE END